D0849950

JMP Connections

Wiley & SAS Business Series

The Wiley & SAS Business Series presents books that help senior-level managers with their critical management decisions.

Titles in the Wiley & SAS Business Series include:

Analytics: The Agile Way by Phil Simon

Analytics in a Big Data World: The Essential Guide to Data Science and Its Applications by Bart Baesens

A Practical Guide to Analytics for Governments: Using Big Data for Good by Marie Lowman

Bank Fraud: Using Technology to Combat Losses by Revathi Subramanian

Big Data Analytics: Turning Big Data into Big Money by Frank Ohlhorst

Big Data, Big Innovation: Enabling Competitive Differentiation through Business Analytics by Evan Stubbs

Business Analytics for Customer Intelligence by Gert Laursen

Business Intelligence Applied: Implementing an Effective Information and Communications Technology Infrastructure by Michael Gendron

Business Intelligence and the Cloud: Strategic Implementation Guide by Michael S. Gendron

Business Transformation: A Roadmap for Maximizing Organizational Insights by Aiman Zeid

Connecting Organizational Silos: Taking Knowledge Flow Management to the Next Level with Social Media by Frank Leistner

Data-Driven Healthcare: How Analytics and BI Are Transforming the Industry by Laura Madsen

Delivering Business Analytics: Practical Guidelines for Best Practice by Evan Stubbs

Demand-Driven Forecasting: A Structured Approach to Forecasting, Second Edition by Charles Chase

Demand-Driven Inventory Optimization and Replenishment: Creating a More Efficient Supply Chain by Robert A. Davis

Developing Human Capital: Using Analytics to Plan and Optimize Your Learning and Development Investments by Gene Pease, Barbara Beresford, and Lew Walker

The Executive's Guide to Enterprise Social Media Strategy: How Social Networks Are Radically Transforming Your Business by David Thomas and Mike Barlow

Economic and Business Forecasting: Analyzing and Interpreting Econometric Results by John Silvia, Azhar Iqbal, Kaylyn Swankoski, Sarah Watt, and Sam Bullard

Economic Modeling in the Post Great Recession Era: Incomplete Data, Imperfect Markets by John Silvia, Azhar Iqbal, and Sarah Watt House

Enhance Oil & Gas Exploration with Data Driven Geophysical and Petrophysical Models by Keith Holdaway and Duncan Irving

Foreign Currency Financial Reporting from Euros to Yen to Yuan: A Guide to Fundamental Concepts and Practical Applications by Robert Rowan

Harness Oil and Gas Big Data with Analytics: Optimize Exploration and Production with Data Driven Models by Keith Holdaway

Health Analytics: Gaining the Insights to Transform Health Care by Jason Burke

Heuristics in Analytics: A Practical Perspective of What Influences Our Analytical World by Carlos Andre Reis Pinheiro and Fiona McNeill

Human Capital Analytics: How to Harness the Potential of Your Organization's Greatest Asset by Gene Pease, Boyce Byerly, and Jac Fitz-enz

Implement, Improve and Expand Your Statewide Longitudinal Data System: Creating a Culture of Data in Education by Jamie McQuiggan and Armistead Sapp

Intelligent Credit Scoring: Building and Implementing Better Credit Risk Scorecards, Second Edition, by Naeem Siddiqi

JMP Connections by John Wubbel

Killer Analytics: Top 20 Metrics Missing from your Balance Sheet by Mark Brown

Machine Learning for Marketers: Hold the Math by Jim Sterne

On-Camera Coach: Tools and Techniques for Business Professionals in a Video-Driven World by Karin Reed

Predictive Analytics for Human Resources by Jac Fitz-enz and John Mattox II

Predictive Business Analytics: Forward-Looking Capabilities to Improve Business Performance by Lawrence Maisel and Gary Cokins

Profit Driven Business Analytics: A Practitioner's Guide to Transforming Big Data into Added Value by Wouter Verbeke, Cristian Bravo, and Bart Baesens

Retail Analytics: The Secret Weapon by Emmett Cox

Social Network Analysis in Telecommunications by Carlos Andre Reis Pinheiro

Statistical Thinking: Improving Business Performance, Second Edition by Roger W. Hoerl and Ronald D. Snee

Strategies in Biomedical Data Science: Driving Force for Innovation by Jay Etchings

Style & Statistic: The Art of Retail Analytics by Brittany Bullard

Taming the Big Data Tidal Wave: Finding Opportunities in Huge Data Streams with Advanced Analytics by Bill Franks

The Analytic Hospitality Executive by Kelly A. McGuire

The Value of Business Analytics: Identifying the Path to Profitability by Evan Stubbs

The Visual Organization: Data Visualization, Big Data, and the Quest for Better Decisions by Phil Simon

Too Big to Ignore: The Business Case for Big Data by Phil Simon

Using Big Data Analytics: Turning Big Data into Big Money by Jared Dean

Win with Advanced Business Analytics: Creating Business Value from Your Data by Jean Paul Isson and Jesse Harriott

For more information on any of the above titles, please visit www.wiley.com.

JMP Connections

The Art of Utilizing Connections
In Your Data

John Wubbel

WILEY

For general information on our other products and services or for technical support, please contact our Customer Care Department within the United States at (800) 762–2974, outside the United States at (317) 572–3993, or fax (317) 572–4002.

Wiley publishes in a variety of print and electronic formats and by print-on-demand. Some material included with standard print versions of this book may not be included in e-books or in print-on-demand. If this book refers to media such as a CD or DVD that is not included in the version you purchased, you may download this material at http://booksupport.wiley.com. For more information about Wiley products, visit www.wiley.com.

Library of Congress Cataloging-in-Publication Data is available:

ISBN 9781119447757 (Hardcover)
ISBN 9781119453741 (ePDF)
ISBN 9781119453727 (ePub)

Cover Design: Wiley
Cover Image: © Thirteen/Shutterstock

Printed in the United States of America.

10 9 8 7 6 5 4 3 2 1

I dedicate this book to my mother and father, my wife Rosmary Wubbel, and son Leslie Wubbel for all their love and support. I especially want to thank three strong ladies, sisters to me for their guidance, care, and constructive comments. Thanks to my best friend and son Leslie for his reviews and the many conversations and topic discussions that helped make this book possible. Thanks to my nieces, especially Catherine Mintmire, for producing the graphic art work. And finally, too numerous to mention the many business friends and mentors in software engineering and data science fields including Philip Douglas Brown for his insights and perspectives on making the connections in data for advancing analytical capabilities.

Contents

List of Figures

Preface

JMP Pro® is the centerpiece software that is capable of saving your business in difficult economic times. JMP CONNECTIONS (herein referred to as "the Model Platform")[1] illustrates the technical means and financial variables that will leverage peak productivity. JMP CONNECTIONS provides a clear pathway toward quickly generating actionable intelligence from your organization's raw data for optimal decision-making purposes. The prime reason for describing a CONNECTIONS platform is the fact that JMP Pro® enables computational in-memory statistical analytical capability second to none in the business, engineering, and scientific world. When a person is able to make a connection, what most often happens is a decision and this fact should generate broad discussion as well as potentially collective performance improvements for groups, teams, or large organizations.

More than ever before, metrics are playing the most important role in the conduct of a business on the competitive stage today. In typical fashion, software comes with a wealth of features, functions, and extensibility. In many cases several software packages may be required to satisfy or facilitate common business functions in support of the operation. Office suites come to mind as an example.

When business conditions are challenging or when strategic goals continually set the bar higher for better performance, innovation is a key factor toward contributing to results that exceed expectations. Consequently, the task of producing metrics must become an innovation as well. As a result, one must visualize a model of capability when it comes to designing, developing, generating, and reporting within your own company, division, or all the way down to the department level. Given the nature of today's office suites, metrics tend to be produced once a week, once a month, or quarterly with

---

[1]The Model Platform describes a Capability Maturity Model supporting the development of Business Intelligence Competency Center for yielding knowledge from data for making optimal decisions in a business enterprise.

each having a cycle time to completion. JMP CONNECTIONS suggests a model, or innovation, that eliminates cycle time so that there is a reduction in full-time equivalents (FTEs) for metric production purposes whereby the metrics produced are real-time or, in other words, "metrics on-demand."

The key to understanding how this type of innovation can lessen tough economic times is through improved business decision making. It is innovative by differentiating between cycle time methods versus metrics that are available with either the latest available data or real-time aggregate raw data material, transformed into usable knowledge.

JMP Pro® is the central hub and can become your command and control center for managing and executing a business operating system on many varied scales. The journey in building a real-time metric production system is simplified through a series of capability maturity steps. Pooling the data from disparate silos starts with data aggregation and integration forming a repository. Mining the repository for conducting statistical analysis, the journey transitions through three levels leading to a final maturity level of predictive modeling and analytic goals. The goals are supportive of the key performance indicators required by the strategic objectives set forth for proper performance management. This book will not only discuss the model but help an organization implement the model with their own people.

CHAPTER 1

Generalized Context for Decision Process Improvement

DECISION PROCESS IMPROVEMENT FOR CORPORATE PERFORMANCE MANAGEMENT

Business is making clear that to stay competitive in the market we need to make decisions quickly and often with disparate data sets. JMP CONNECTIONS should be viewed as a business-oriented data discovery tool and is not an information technology (IT) or enterprise SAP®[1] Centric model because as is so often the case, data sets are not under the control of the IT department. Data may reside in silos, dozens of spreadsheets, or proprietary database applications. Thus, we can best describe this exercise as the "decision process improvement." If we can improve on the way metrics are produced, it can directly improve the timely implementation of actual decisions for corporate performance management.

The Holy Grail of the Information Age particularly in the information technology (IT) shop is the notion of data integration and interoperability. The Institute of Electrical and Electronics Engineers defines *interoperability* as:

> The ability of two or more systems or components to exchange information and to use the information that has been exchanged.

Unfortunately, interoperability has never been entirely achieved across a large enterprise before.

However, in support of staying competitive, the popular business press and IT periodicals have been pushing "business intelligence" (BI). Business intelligence is a broad category of applications and technologies for gathering, storing, analyzing, and providing access to data to help enterprise users make better business decisions.

---

[1] SAP stands for Systeme, Andwendungen, Produkte in der Datenverarbeitung, which, translated to English, means Systems, Applications, Products in data processing.

As postulated in the Preface, a tough economy implies a propensity to cut back on expenditures across a wide cross section of the enterprise that may also include BI software acquisitions. Utilizing JMP Pro®, the following pages will show precisely how the development of state-of-the-art metrics can be facilitated without the need for a major capital expenditure (CAPEX) project.

1.1 SITUATIONAL ASSESSMENT (CURRENT STATE)

ADVANCEMENT IN METRICS FOR BUSINESS AUGMENTATION

Before describing the common state of affairs that may be typical from small to large businesses, a framework for visualizing capability maturity with regard to the development of metrics and their use is outlined in Figure 1.1.

0. The lowest level of capability maturity (Level 0) would be a business or organization that may not have an IT department. Most of the management and reporting of business data is done using spreadsheets and perhaps the facilities of software office suites/applications for presentations. Reporting may be ad hoc or sporadic due to such factors as data that is not readily in a form for use in conducting statistical analysis when required. Companies often have so much data that they realize knowledge is locked up; however, they have no practical, inexpensive way to develop and utilize it.

1. The first level of maturity (Level 1) is where companies produce dashboards, scorecards, and KPIs on a regular basis. Perhaps on an annual basis, metrics are reviewed for relevance as needs change over time. Metrics retained may be refined and presentation and timely delivery mechanisms are *level set*[2] depending on who is to be receiving them and at what levels of the enterprise they are to be receiving and using them. Publishing BI tools like dashboards (DBs) and scorecards (SCs) have measurable cycle times.

---

[2]A situation in which everyone in a group has a basic understanding of a situation.

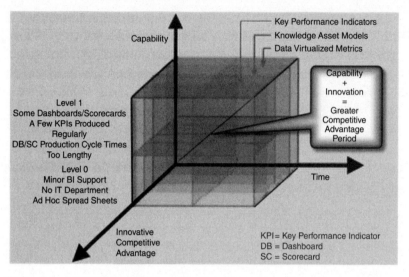

Figure 1.1 JMP CONNECTIONS Capability Maturity Model Levels 0 and 1

2. The second level of maturity (Level 2) for an organization would be a realization that some subset of deliverable metrics could be converted to metrics "on-demand." In identifying these on-demand metrics, the cycle time to generate or refresh a set of deliverable dashboards would be completely eliminated. (See Figure 1.2.)

3. The third and highest level of maturity (Level 3) is a two-part configuration. (See Figure 1.2.)

Level 3, Part 1

■ Eliminate cycle time to create on-demand metrics resulting in reduction in FTEs.

Level 3, Part 2

■ Human capital resource reallocation for:
    ■ Performing advanced statistical analysis
    ■ Predictive analytics and modeling

Level 3, Part 1, maturity level, focuses on reducing the time it takes (cycle time) to produce the metrics on a scheduled basis,

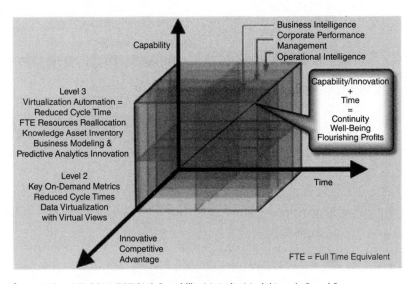

Figure 1.2   JMP CONNECTIONS Capability Maturity Model Levels 2 and 3

thus in turn reducing the number of FTEs required to produce those metrics. One FTE required to update a dashboard every week does not leave enough time for any other production tasks for metrics. The amount of time for an FTE is finite. As hours are freed up, other knowledge within the data sets can be developed and utilized. Achieving the second level of maturity leads into Level 3, Part 2 because now predictive analytics and the full power of JMP Pro can be leveraged perhaps without the addition of more FTEs. The graphic view in Figure 1.3 summarizes the reference model for maturity capability for business intelligence metrics.

The development of JMP CONNECTIONS is applicable to literally every type of business. All examples cited in this book are totally fictional and for illustrative purposes, which can be adapted to any business. The examples are generic in the sense that the common fuel crucial to business execution is the enterprise data, mature knowledge assets, and performance indicators across the spectrum of organizations that desire optimal results. In many circumstances, particularly in larger firms, one expects to find whatever data they need on the large enterprise database applications. In fact, the information is out there but its access is less than ideal. It may in no way be in a

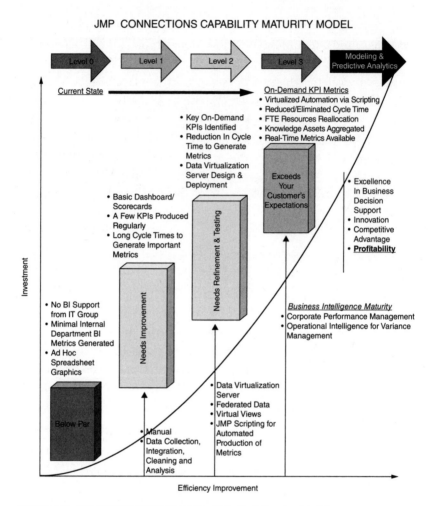

Figure 1.3 JMP CONNECTIONS Capability Maturity Reference Model

format to provide any statistical analysis capability. It lacks a certain agility for manipulative processes for generating BI tools or data. It is a "what you see is what you get" due to the hard-coded requirements built into the application. Consequently, a query returned is often a table of data or records that do not necessarily communicate or impart knowledge to the recipient. Something extra needs to be done.

Additionally, one would think that, especially within technology firms or scientific and engineering firms, data management would be state of the art. For many and perhaps for a majority, business is conducted using spreadsheets, small desktop database applications, web applications, text files, and sticky notes. In fact, the proliferation of spreadsheets from one year to the next with no sense of version control is prevalent where many sheets act as placeholders for data rather than actually doing any computations or analysis.

Given the standard corporate desktop environment, when a set of metrics are required, they are likely prepared using a combination of the office suite applications. These may include the word processor, spreadsheet, and presentation software applications. A chart or graph may be present with some annotation explaining the meaning of the numbers and is the bare minimum or Level 0 of maturity for making metrics. Thus, it is useful to point out here exactly what types of BI solutions exist.

1. Executive scorecards and dashboards
2. Online Analytical Processing (OLAP) analysis
3. Ad hoc reporting
4. Operational reporting
5. Forecasting
6. Data mining
7. Customer intelligence

Each of the BI solutions has a data analysis ingredient or function that derives the reported out metric for a particular BI solution. While features and functions may be alike, what sets these apart is how they are applied to support decision making.

To be more precise in thinking about analytic metrics, there are three areas of data analysis derived from data science, information technology, and business applications that can be categorized as follows:

* PREDICTIVE (Forecasting)
* DESCRIPTIVE (Business Intelligence and Data Mining)
* PRESCRIPTIVE (Modeling, Optimization, and Simulation)

Without efficient sharing of operational business intelligence, a company is going to suffer breakdowns from small to large, be unable to properly grow, and could even be flirting with massive disaster. A small issue, for example, can escalate into something very large very quickly if there's not good sharing of business intelligence. No operational intelligence, or incorrect intelligence, means that a company will create and execute strategies and plans (i.e., make decisions) that could inadvertently be bad for the company.

Beyond the Level 3 capability maturity, one may begin to get a sense about the concept of a BI Competency Center. A competency center is inclusive of all three areas when it comes to data analysis—PREDICTIVE, DESCRIPTIVE, and PRESCRIPTIVE—with respect to applying BI solutions to support various decision-making units within the enterprise. The competency center concept also can act as a facilitator for efficiently sharing operational business intelligence.

■ PREDICTIVE

Even though the word *predict* is embedded in the notion of predictive analytics with inference toward trending and forecasting, the proper application of predictive analytics can also provide an essential competitive edge with regard to what is going to happen in the next minute, hour, or day. Consequently, our concepts of *on-demand and real-time metrics* are synonymous. An example of metrics on-demand is in Section 3.6, on page 80, Metric Case Study. A preview here of the case study illustrates how predictive analytics can be used by the maintenance department for real-time *business service management* (BSM). What is BSM? Simply, it means one department that provides services to another within a corporate enterprise. Business service management is an approach used in information technology departments to manage business aligned with IT services. In the case study, BSM is the relationship the maintenance department has with supporting manufacturing in a factory. On the shop floor of a factory, maintenance services are essential for operational efficiency. Alignment for one department makes sense when maintenance is interested in predicting machine part failures or determining the optimal time to do preventative maintenance that should be conducted for minimizing downtime in the factory.

■ DESCRIPTIVE

In a Focus Factory[3] manufacturing model, real-time metrics are essentially *operational business intelligence* where information is used on a daily basis to run production. Thus, the word *descriptive* implies it is the knowledge of the factory's contiguity (i.e., the "state of being"). To determine the cooperation of entities (e.g., persons) with equipment or to monitor the usage of equipment, whether good, bad, or steady state, for example, in a focus factory model, is to know the operational condition or situation for a given period of time.

Performance issues will be directly related to the type of metrics used to support specific areas of the factory. Measures will typically be at a more granular level. Current dashboard and scorecard metrics will reflect the higher level results and aggregate productivity measures.

■ PRESCRIPTIVE

The *prescriptive* kinds of metric examples are the types conducted prior to the introduction of a new process—the design of experiment statistical modeling to establish, for example, critical parameters and limits.

While having enumerated the types of BI above, none of these are inexpensive for companies finding themselves in uncertain economic situations. With commercial applications, no one size fits all and few at the retail level in the marketplace for commercial applications understand the level of data integration required. Data integration and its implementation is not generic or available off-the-shelf. Data integration enables interoperability across the enterprise, which is directly related to capability. In other words, the more integrated the data, the better the operability, which translates into a higher level of capability when utilized. With JMP CONNECTIONS, a lower granularity of data aggregation and subsequent integration is possible. (Granularity means a finely detailed but not necessarily more voluminous amount of data.) Granularity may be more desirable to go from a generalized metric to something more specific. Together, the data integration,

---

[3]The term *focused factory* was introduced in a 1974 *Harvard Business Review* article authored by Wickham Skinner [32].

data definition/description language (i.e., may use a declarative syntax to define fields and data types), and selection steps using the structured query language (i.e., using a collection of imperative verbs) for the codified business logic, collectively, should strive to produce only the minimal data set required to perform any analysis and the final metric presentation.

At the lowest level of maturity (Level 0), many key performance metrics are produced with a great deal of effort. Effort in effect means the non-automated tasks required from data gathering to finished presentations. From start to finish the cycle time for such efforts is associated with a (Level 0) maturity capability. The non-automated process of making a metric is the manual work done by hand and, when performed repeatedly, the business logic that goes into it is unconsciously executed by the analyst. The manual effort and repeatable business logic required is measured as cycle time in the generation of metrics. In order to reduce the cycle time, the manual work has to be off-loaded to the computer. To eliminate the manual work, the business logic is codified as Structured Query Language statements for retrieving data from the Data Virtualization Server (DVS) so that it can be acted upon by JMP. The business logic can also be written into JMP scripts for execution within JMP prerequisite for any analysis. If the metric is not a one of a kind or ad hoc production and is required periodically by management, the codification thereby reduces or eliminates the cycle time required to produce the metric by doing away with mundane manual tasks. More details regarding the technical aspects will follow in Chapter 2—Real-Time Metrics Business Case.

Even with the best visual presentations, graphical layout and designs offered by the office suites appear acceptable, but they are less than optimal compared to JMP visualization metrics. Third-party BI applications may require extensive programming to achieve even a partial analytic capacity. Unlike with JMP, the current state of an organization at a maturity Level 0 with basic office suites is challenged to perform any statistical analysis. A good place to start for an organization to understand where they are in terms of where they are on the capability reference model is to write a clear and concise problem statement that can guide them forward from (Level 0) through (Level 3) on their Decision Improvement Process journey.

1.2 PROBLEM STATEMENT

COMPETENCY CENTER METRICS ON-DEMAND

A problem statement is a description of the issue at hand. It includes a vision, issue statement, and a method to solve the problem. The problem statement below expresses in words the effort and focus it will take to achieve the task and represents a solve-able problem.

The primary problem is to be able to journey from a (Level 0) maturity level to the (Level 2) capability. The transition from the current state to the "metrics on-demand" basis is a realization of the following:

1. More realistic view of current state/transitions in support of corporate strategic goals
2. Savings realized via reduced FTE hours for developing metrics
3. Potential redeployed human resources
4. More precise and reliable metrics
5. Higher quality of decision making possible
6. Better utilization of additional knowledge
7. Realizing an inventory of "knowledge capital" from the knowledge assets developed
8. Innovation in delivery methods and timeliness

As with most problems, certain assumptions go with the territory. These include the following:

1. A department or organization is already generating periodic business intelligence.
2. The current metrics do not or cannot answer extemporaneous questions.
3. The customer or end user has a sense of latency about the timely receipt of the metrics.
4. There is no business intelligence competency center across the enterprise for establishing standards.
5. The metrics may or may not support corporate initiatives.
6. Data integrity may be less than perfect.

While on the journey transitioning through each maturity level, the organization at some point should establish a Business Intelligence Competency Center (BICC). There are several factors that make this idea lucrative. The mind map in Figure 1.4 is representative in the context of bringing metrics through the levels of maturity that is simply not employing just any person(s) or group(s) of people, rather a center of excellence dedicated to the development and production of business intelligence metrics as part of the value-added piece to this innovative work.

Large businesses typically have multiple departments. Many of the departments are creating metrics and there is often duplication of work. Knowing where these duplicate work efforts exist is a target for becoming lean (improve efficiency and productivity and reduce waste), resulting in substantial savings. When there are several groups producing similar metrics, there can be ambiguity with respect to the meaning of the resulting data. The BI competency center should be the "go-to" group for enterprise organizations to get their key performance metrics. There are solid reasons for taking this approach. The competency center can establish standards and guidelines for producing metrics with consistency. In other words the inputs and outputs can be validated. Given that so many companies are dealing with legacy applications, database servers, and assorted data silos, the competency center can resolve data ambiguity between systems. Developing and maintaining an ontology could be appropriate in some cases. In other words, a glossary or vocabulary defining the terms that are common for metrics and unique for a particular business facilitates better communication between people when discussing or analyzing metrics.

At the Level 1 maturity, working up the metrics entails the aggregation of data. In other words, a certain amount of cycle time is used up in gathering that data from different silos, repositories, and exportable resources. Prior to doing any statistical analysis may require data integration work. It is very common that to compute a KPI, data comes from two different resources and must be combined. Much of that work might be using some information from a spreadsheet, information from an SAP application resource exported to a spreadsheet, and a cross reference to another database table. The integration effort might include writing some spreadsheet macros and using lookup

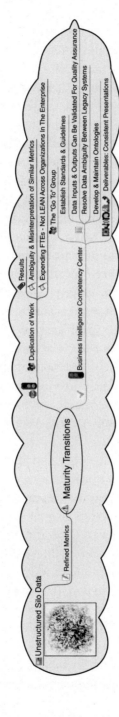

Figure 1.4 Maturity through Level State Transitions

13

functions simply to get to a point where a chart can be generated. Many customized requests for metrics are not available from the large enterprise applications because the data used in operations may only be local and owned by the department.

The person doing the metrics is familiar with and is perhaps the subject matter expert (SME) of raw data. His or her feel or sense about the data, where it comes from and how it is entered, is more acute and is evident when it comes to such things as questionable data, values, or the semantic context from which it is derived in the business. Because of this awareness, along with integration, data may need to be cleaned by a summary review. Does a certain record or data item make sense? When something does not look right or an outlier is seen that is normally not the case, the cycle time to create the metric is expanded due to the fact that one has to investigate the validity of a single data point. The data might have been incorrectly entered, missed, or is of the wrong type or format. Data integrity issues are typical when multiple people are entering data into spreadsheets where entries cannot be validated. These are known as errors, are very subtle, and are missed "right first time" opportunities.

To understand the problem statement, outside of living at the Level 1 maturity space, describing the environment aids us in defining a better way toward achieving the next level of capability. A simple but not uncommon development cycle, Figure 1.5 depicts a current Level 1 maturity state.

The entire cycle time to completely update a set of dashboard slides for presentation from start to finish on a weekly basis is a limitation. It is a limitation due to the fact that a person has at most 40 hours per week, leaving no time to accomplish other tasks or improve on the ways he or she works. No new metrics can be researched, designed, and deployed under these circumstances. A good example of time consumed would be the manual effort to include the query of a third-party database application, using an export template to extract that data into a spreadsheet, followed by any statistical analysis required that needs to be conducted in JMP in order to complete the dashboard development cycle.

In summary, recognition of the problem is a statement elucidating the current state in contrast to a usable set of metrics that are literally

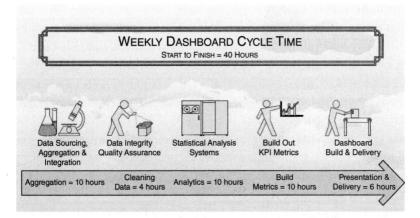

Figure 1.5 Common Cycle Time to Build and Publish a Weekly Dashboard

available at our fingertips at any time. Reaching the pinnacle of real-time metrics is a series of steps or transition processes that comes by solving these problems and turning them into the equity of competence, a combination of knowledge, skills, and behavior used to improve performance.

1.3 VISUALIZING STATE TRANSITION

REACTIVE DECISION MAKING, PROACTIVE DECISIONS

In the previous section, the generalization of moving among the various maturity capability levels is a process of steps within a level as well as between levels. To abstract the actions of transiting from one to the other, one way to visualize states and the transitions is through a state table. A state table is essentially a truth table in which some of the inputs are the current state, and the outputs include the next state. To make this concept less abstract, theoretical computer science makes use of state transition tables in automata theory[4] and sequential logic. There are a number of tables, one-dimensional and

---

[4]We leave it to the reader to explore advanced readings in automata theory, mathematical models, and problem solving.

two-dimensional, and from these state diagrams can be sketched. However, in this section, visualizing the transitions and resulting transformations, the discussion will be more about the tangibles the analyst has to deal with and not about the theory. The theory of state transition gives us a general context or model to think about or to intellectualize the mechanics. The tangible factors are the tools, resources, and manual tasks that could be called the practical state the analyst finds at the beginning and throughout the journey in building the JMP CONNECTIONS platform.

Assuming metrics "on-demand" is a more desirable state based on the notion that the immediacy is more relevant particularly in terms of decreasing reactive decision making, certain things must happen in transition. First, a metric must have some measure of repeatability and thereby lend itself to some degree of automation for reproduction purposes. If the computer can replicate the manual labor involved in producing the end product of user accepted KPIs, then we can see our way through toward reducing the hours for an FTE to do the same, in other words shrinkage of the cycle time to produce each metric.

Data aggregation is another time-consuming component within the cycle time. There are a number of ways to render aggregation out of the cycle time equation. First and foremost, JMP provisions a wide variety of connectivity methods that can be optimized for tapping data resources. These include the following:

1. A default feature, access to JMP tables
2. Electronic serial data connectivity to instrumentation
3. Microsoft Excel® spreadsheet importation
4. JMP Excel Add-In and Profiler
5. Database connectivity via ODBC drivers and SQL interface
6. Uniform Resource Locator (URL) via http protocol through JMP
7. Connectivity to SAS and SAS databases

JMP CONNECTIONS may be analogous to open pit quarry mining [22] because mineral wealth may be exposed at the multiple layers of geological formations. Data mining can expose a wealth of knowledge and opportunity with connectivity options.

The oldest form of connectivity in the data processing world and supported by JMP is using a serial/null modem cable or modem with communications software to connect to a device whereby the device is sending or streaming data that may be useful in monitoring a piece of equipment. JMP documentation and sample code are available for this type of connectivity.

Spreadsheets can be imported as well; however, sometimes there are issues with the data in regards to type, format, and qualitative interpretation. JMP Add-In functions facilitate a two-way data pathway between JMP and spreadsheet data. Spreadsheets can be representative of the data as though it were located in a database table. The only limitation is the fact that it cannot be queried like a database using Structured Query Language. It is a straight open-file operation that brings the sheet into a JMP table.

Database connectivity is the most flexible in terms of access to most commercial and open source database servers due to the fact that ODBC drivers are available for different data source types, connection information, and credentials for access. It is also the most powerful in allowing the BI developer to query only for an exact data set across more than one table.

The URL connection also provisions a whole new bevy of options for garnering data for use in JMP. Public domain data sets available on the World Wide Web or on intranet systems opens up a whole new resource. While JMP does not give you access to real-time streaming data, say for example from an automated manufacturing machine, there may be other innovative ways to retain the data. The JMP Pro Version 11 Scripting Guide, Chapter 14, Extending JMP, states that real-time data capture from a device is possible through the serial port. In the semiconductor industry, electronic test equipment such as a logic analyzer will be capable of dumping data to the serial port. A JMP datafeed object will enable a connection to the data, capture the data, and utilize the data with background event processing.

For example, manufacturing execution systems (MESs) today are generally automated, and consequently terabytes of data can come streaming from production floor equipment while in operation such as from (PLC) controllers, sensors, and temperature and humidity probes to name a few.

Many manufacturing firms use historian systems for management of real-time data and events coming from production equipment. With a historian system implemented in a large manufacturing production floor environment, data may stream so fast that it is more practical to catch and compress the data for storage typically in a proprietary format as opposed to storage into a relational database. The data may later be stored in a database for analysis and accessed via JMP. One type of application here would be to monitor equipment for reliability and dynamically create control charts to monitor performance for overall equipment effectiveness (OEE).

With these connectivity options, a certain amount of creativity can go a long way. The multitudinous connections with JMP as the centerpoint of all these potential component parts works in favor of aggregation.

In practice, and as a matter of practicality, departments often find themselves awash in a sea of spreadsheets. The practicality is to reduce the number of spreadsheets. But how can you reduce the number of spreadsheets when people need the data they contain? Even though JMP can access data in spreadsheets, there still exists a gap with regard to optimal aggregation when data is stored in disparate places. This fact hinders the ability to completely arrive at a Level 2 capability. Hindrances include difficulties in coding or scripting logic that yields the automation for lowering FTE hours required through the cycle time reduction for producing the metric. Without a complete aggregation, data integration is not possible for data sets that remain in their mini-silos and are lost opportunities with respect to graduating this data from an unstructured state to structured data where the integration opens new data discovery opportunities. Another way to think about this situation is when the data remains in silos, one can only have a single-dimensional view. Once the data is aggregated, multidimensional views become available. Disconnected data is simply inefficient.

To effectively overcome this roadblock to attaining a balanced and near-total aggregation of data from your inventory of spreadsheets is really quite simple. The solution will be discussed with details in Chapter 2.

The final concept to transition from a Level 1 to a Level 2 capability are the data discovery opportunities that come out of the data

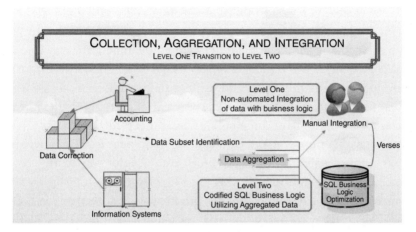

Figure 1.6 Transition from Level 1 to Level 2

integration step. To refresh, during the Level 1 cycle time there are many instances where the integration of collected data is also a manual task to get to a graphic or KPI. (See Figure 1.6.)

In the JMP CONNECTION scenario, it is very easy to prototype the abstraction of integration, for example, via structured query language statements from a database connection where SQL JOIN commands can pull from multiple tables. In fact, a useful database feature is creating a VIEW which is a virtual table. One does not have to recreate these week after week. The database server maintains a VIEW so they can be brought into JMP via the ODBC execution of SQL or running a JMP script that opens the database connection, reads in the table, processes the statistical analytics, and generates final output in one stroke.

Data integration at this point may take only as much time as you are currently spending on a metric within your Level 1 cycle time. However, once aggregation is defined and becomes available, more time developing data integration may result as new insights become apparent. This outcome is a direct benefit of automating to a real-time metric delivery system.

Visualizing the progress, state transitions, and the transformation across the levels of maturity capability, both in theory and in practice, keeps development on the right path and on track. The current state, new inputs, actions followed by outputs, and acceptance from old state to a new state is a way to think about the quality of your work and avoid any superfluous metrics as well as non-value-added work on the project. The simple analogy of a closed or finite state machine is that of a door. If you build a door, the initial state is open. The transition happens when it closes and its final state is a door that is closed. When someone takes the action to enter through the door, it transitions to the open state. If the builder did not get the door jam square upon hanging the door, and closing it the door jams, then somewhere in the construction either some work was not done or in this case some non-value-added work was done incorrectly. As long as we are concerned about efficiency, higher productivity, and better decisions through metrics, we might as well maintain a realistic vision about our JMP CONNECTIONS work in order to obtain the goal of business intelligence competency.

1.4 METRICS ON-DEMAND

EXCEED CUSTOMER EXPECTATIONS = BEST-IN-CLASS METRICS

The Best-in-class Metrics is a Business Intelligence Competency Center with the implication that the best metrics produced is the objective to satisfy the mission to exceed customer expectations. The rate of change at which we approach best-in-class status is a function of the ability to reduce the production cycle time of metrics and in turn FTEs. The mind map in Figure 1.7 is a point of reference for the next discussion about factors involved to exceed customer expectations.

The transition to metrics on-demand may be incremental as an organization moves to the Level 2 capability. Recall, the purpose of developing through the Level 2 virtualized deployment of data is not to supplant other major enterprise systems; rather it is preferable to be operating on local data that is not under the control of the IT department. Granted, this platform model might be pulling subsets of data from various enterprise resources, but people within the organization or various departments will be using the resultant metrics in their own unique ways to support their mission.

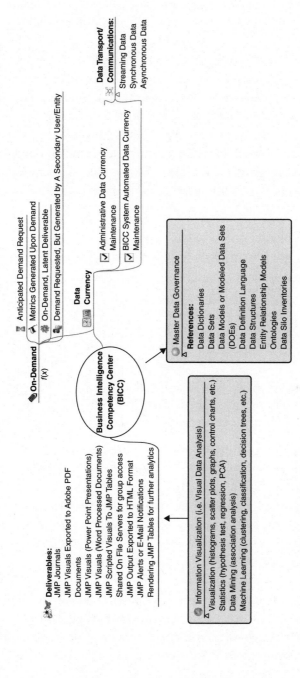

On-Demand

f(x)

- Anticipated Demand Request
- Metrics Generated Upon Demand
- On-Demand, Latent Deliverable
- Demand Requested, But Generated by A Secondary User/Entity

Deliverables:
JMP Journals
JMP Visuals Exported to Adobe PDF
Documents
JMP Visuals (Power Point Presentations)
JMP Visuals (Word Processed Documents)
JMP Scripted Visuals To JMP Tables
Shared On File Servers for group access
JMP Output Exported to HTML Format
JMP Alerts or E-Mail Notifications
Rendering JMP Tables for further analytics

Data Currency

- Administrative Data Currency Maintenance
- BICC System Automated Data Currency Maintenance

Business Intelligence Competency Center (BICC)

- Master Data Governance
- **References:**
  Data Dictionaries
  Data Sets
  Data Models or Modeled Data Sets
  (DOEs)
  Data Definition Language
  Data Structures
  Entity Relationship Models
  Ontologies
  Data Silo Inventories

- Information Visualization (i.e. Visual Data Analysis)
- Visualization (histograms, scatter plots, graphs, control charts, etc.)
  Statistics (hypothesis test, regression, PCA)
  Data Mining (association analysis)
  Machine Learning (clustering, classification, decision trees, etc.)

Data Transport/ Communications:
Streaming Data
Synchronous Data
Asynchronous Data

Figure 1.7   Achieving On-Demand Capability

Achieving on-demand capability requires three attentive considerations. First and most obvious is that raw data must be maintained and up to date or kept as current as possible. This task is most demanding when harvesting from various silos of data. For example, when JMP has no access to an external database application, alternatively one is required to export data sets. Additional steps might be involved to aggregate the data from the silo into the local database repository. In Section 2.1, the aggregation of data from many silos into a local database as a small warehouse will be discussed.

A secondary consideration involves the planning on how the metrics are going to be delivered once JMP is able to provide finished output. With JMP CONNECTIONS, there are many options available as follows:

1. JMP journals.
2. JMP add-in for rolling visuals into Adobe® PDF or Microsoft PowerPoint® presentations.
3. Save JMP scripts to JMP tables for later reruns.
4. Incorporate into JMP scripts embedding graphics into word processor files.
5. Saving to Adobe Flash SWF files.
6. Locating JMP output to shared file servers for group access.
7. Incorporating into JSL, JMP output can go directly to a web server for online delivery for web browsing.

In most cases, end-user customers will probably dictate how and where they want to see the metrics, and so a combination of options will likely be put into practice. How the presentation is deployed can be easier if one can anticipate the end-user requirements.

Finally, the metric currency of data with regard to its suitable timeliness is a question that will be asked. Metrics on-demand implies that when a customer asks for it, either the metric has to have already been generated with the latest data available or the metric is generated immediately upon the demand request with minimal latency to delivery. Does the system automatically maintain currency or are there times where either an administrator or end user invokes regeneration for a metric? The answer to this question really depends on the data. There are three factors that may drive how data currency is resolved as follows:

1. Streaming data
2. Periodic or synchronous data
3. Ad hoc (aka, asynchronous) data

Data that may be arriving as a stream may require a constant refresh, for example, monitoring the performance of a machine. Periodic data may arrive at specific intervals to the system, therefore generating the metric, and remaining current may only occur on a periodic basis as well. Ad hoc data comes into the system at unpredictable times. In order to maintain a current metric one might have to rely on the system to detect the event and run a batch or cron (i.e., scheduled) job in the background to update output for the customer. A cron job is simply a time-based job or task scheduler that uses a table or crontab containing the command for each job to run at a specific time. Each of these scenarios is a technical decision that factors into the presentation delivery design, implementation, and deployment task.

Presentation formats and means of delivery should be as automated as possible since the actual presentation is recognized as a component of cycle time at the Level 1 capability. In order to eliminate cycle time, which is the key factor in achieving Level 2 capability, if the computer system upon which this model is implemented can perform these tasks and it becomes a feature of the JMP CONNECTIONS system, the savings is a huge benefit for everyone. And just like the data aggregation and integration, once put in place one does not have to come back week after week to perform some manual task prior to producing the desired KPIs.

As the Level 2 capability incrementally comes online, less time can be devoted to cyclic output for metrics and more time spent developing new knowledge from the data now under your control. For example, what may materialize is the ability to validate data and run exception reports to identify anomalies. Catching issues or defects in methods or processes early can equate to a higher level of quality assurance and great savings.

Real-Time Metrics Business Case

Sometimes the lure of technology overshadows reason. Regardless of where one finds and may perceive improvements to the way a firm produces the metrics necessary to run an efficient operation, a business case must be developed to justify expenditures in time and money to upgrade. In addition, writing a business case is an opportunity to analyze the feasibility in a structured manner and whether it can be successfully accomplished in tough economic environments. (See Figure 2.1.)

In Chapter 2, a basic/generic case model that stimulates the thinking behind JMP CONNECTIONS is illustrative and does not need to be overly complex. The various sections include the Project Description and Objectives, a Solution, Cost and Benefit Analysis, Financial Assessment, Implementation Timeline, Critical Assumptions and Risk Assessment, and Recommendations.

Indisputably, industry and market competition is amplified well above what it was in previous years. Simply working harder is not going to keep us competitive. Competitors are using the latest statistical software packages and automated tools representing a competitive threat because they are not going to grow market share; they are going to be working to take your market share away. Therefore, we need

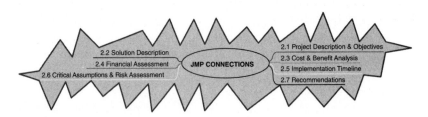

Figure 2.1 Business Case Basics

to strive for perfection in our production operations by using the best metrics, analytic methods, and utilization at all levels. Leveraging the knowledge bound within our volumes of data is the key to success. Let's go forward with a solid business case.

2.1 PROJECT DESCRIPTION AND OBJECTIVES—A CASE STUDY

RESOURCE EXPLOITABLE DATA FOR KEY PERFORMANCE INDICATORS

This fictional project is a data management initiative to aggregate data into a database as a data micro-warehouse[1] with JMP retrofitted front end for statistical analysis and reporting for real-time operational management and decision support. The objective is to eliminate the process and associated cycle time to produce key performance indicators as delivered in dashboards, scorecards, and other reporting mechanisms. (See Figures 2.2 and 2.3.) Systematic measurement should monitor progress and quantify improvement, savings, efficiency, and gains. Target objectives are:

1. To reduce the number of static spreadsheets
2. Remediate identified RFT opportunities with data input
3. Integration
4. Management activities

Achieving these objectives must result in less time spent working to pull the data together, giving people more time to review, study, and analyze reported KPIs and associated metrics.

The project commences with the building of a working prototype developed from current manual methods of producing metrics. The process ends with the automated real-time output of business intelligence generated from codified business logic located between the data micro-warehouse[2] and the JMP statistical package. The codified

---

[1] The term *micro-warehouse* will be defined in Chapter 3.
[2] Micro-warehouse also means any other potential JMP connectivity opportunity such as access to an automation historian system where JMP can utilize real-time data/data feeds for monitoring processes or produce documentation for deviation investigations.

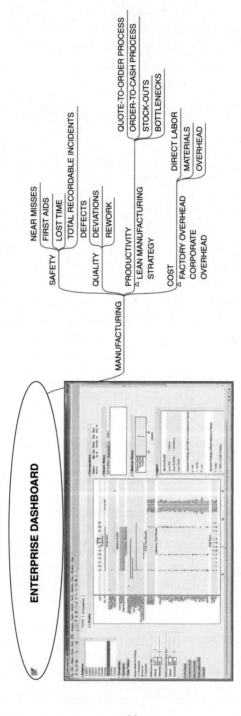

ENTERPRISE DASHBOARD

MANUFACTURING

SAFETY
NEAR MISSES
FIRST AIDS
LOST TIME
TOTAL RECORDABLE INCIDENTS

QUALITY
DEFECTS
DEVIATIONS
REWORK

PRODUCTIVITY
△ LEAN MANUFACTURING
STRATEGY
QUOTE-TO-ORDER PROCESS
ORDER-TO-CASH PROCESS
STOCK-OUTS
BOTTLENECKS

COST
△ FACTORY OVERHEAD
CORPORATE
OVERHEAD
DIRECT LABOR
MATERIALS
OVERHEAD

Figure 2.2   Dashboard [29]

28

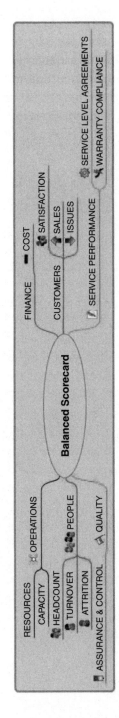

Figure 2.3 Balanced Scorecard

logic is (SQL) statements. The data aggregation process is to bring the data from various silos, repositories like spreadsheets, and third-party database applications and introduce data sets into the warehouse. The SQL represents the data integration of components or data subsets rolled into the business logic that generates the input into the JMP. JMP produces the visual graphics and reports facilitating statistical analytics where appropriate. The end users include potentially any-one involved in operations. The factory generates volumes of raw data. Converting data into meaningful metrics functions to support management and decision support in the business operating system.

Any system that has potential connectivity to JMP would be considered for inclusion into the project. Systems that supply timely data to the micro-warehouse for read-only purposes contribute to the system. Those systems are excluded for writing or updating since the JMP CONNECTION platform is not a transaction-based system.

Success will be measured based on the performance gains coming from the production floor. The success is critical with the duty to always be thinking about what the success metric should be. People do not typ-ically make any correlations between having the right data and being a success. Thinking about the success metric also means that you should be able to demonstrate that success and the realized performance gains are due to these metrics. An example of a way to demonstrate a suc-cess is to actually show results so there is a connection that people can relate the metric to the enhanced ability to make a better business decision at key decision points, or, how the metric allows a team to collectively perform better. It is the success concept that people are not able to put their finger on and thus is the realization that the newfound knowledge from this data is what is making the difference between mediocrity or resounding success. If the connections between what should be measured, monitored, analyzed, and acted upon were easy to identify, people probably would have been eager for it sooner. And there are those people who know in an organization what those nice-to-have metrics are, but it is often an impossible task to gener-ate in a cost-effective manner. In other words one would spend more to make the metric than is actually realized in savings. Making the connections in your data makes it much easier once the JMP CON-NECTIONS platform is in place.

2.2 SOLUTION DESCRIPTION

COMPETENCY CENTER FOR BUSINESS INTELLIGENCE

The solution strives to be the Business Intelligence Competency Center for operations. An idealized competency center could be described as the aggregate sum total of all metrics produced for business operations such that the view of this world is a Virtual Production Control Room. Two aspects of competency are the consolidation of data into single repository and beginning the process of defining ontologies. An ontology formally represents knowledge as a set of concepts within a domain, and the relationships between pairs of concepts.

It is appropriate to note here that as data is virtualized, brought together via aggregation and integrated, it is easy to start thinking about the need for master data management (MDM) followed by terms such as *metadata*. Developing the company's master data and defining descriptive metadata, or data that describes data, may necessarily be a precursor step toward realizing formal ontologies. The management aspect of MDM though is a set of processes, governance, policies, standards, and tools that consistently defines a means to manage master data where non-transactional data entities in an organization include reference data. The objective of MDM can be described as providing processes for collecting, aggregating, matching, consolidating, and quality-assuring for persistence and distributing such data throughout an enterprise. The idea is to ensure consistency and control in the ongoing maintenance and use of such data by applications. MDM begs again the question and desire to have true interoperability as discussed earlier, particularly between different machines and applications where the need to share data is patently obvious. While in the context of developing the JMP CONNECTIONS platform, MDM development may be viewed as an intermediate transition step. Many firms go no further once their MDM work is done and only require maintenance. Later it will be shown how and why an ontology becomes important for converting data into actionable intelligence.

An ontology can be explained with a very technical description, or formally bound into a Resource Description Framework file or visually and diagrammatically. A very basic introduction for the reader would be a couple of small classic ontologies considered "good ontologies" found at the W3C Organization (http://www.w3.org/wiki/Good_ Ontologies) listing the Dublin Core (DC) Ontology, Friend of a Friend (FOAF), Socially Interconnected Online Communities (SIOC), the Good Relations Ontology, and The Music Ontology.

More important than understanding the technical nature is knowing why an organization would want to develop an ontology for a competency center. At Stanford University, McGuinness and Noy list some reasons as follows [26]:

- To enable reuse of domain knowledge
- To make domain assumptions explicit
- To analyze domain knowledge
- To separate domain knowledge from operational knowledge
- To share common understanding of the structure of information among people or software agents

Realize that across the entire range in the journey to build out the JMP CONNECTION platform, one is organizing structure. Building out is structuring unstructured data, creating business logic, or formalizing relationships with data, people, processes, machinery, and so on. If a company is not mature in using BI metrics, most likely there is no enterprise architecture framework in place which defines how to organize the structure and views associated with the enterprise. As KPIs are identified and the micro-warehouse repository comes to life, things start to sort out as to which knowledge domain the metrics belong. Ontologies are the structural frameworks for organizing information about the world or some part of it. What might be the ultimate frontier for the BICC from a virtual control room concept is the integrated knowledge environment whereby ontologies are a component of an open semantic enterprise for knowledge management and representation.

Thus far, describing the JMP CONNECTION platform as a model of data virtualization is an exercise in structural integration of data resources, warehousing, and analysis. Integrating semantic mechanisms can make a big difference in friendly and adaptive interaction use cases when it comes to the deployment of BI. Ontologies-based integration is the link between the structural and semantic integration that has the potential yield of transforming the practical workspace into a virtual business-oriented analysis world in which business-people expect to be working. Further, introducing the concept of integration may lead to a unification of knowledge assets in the enterprise as a portal for all BI packages that develop on the platform.

For context, a graphical business example of an ontology is given here (Figure 2.4). The following example is taken from the book titled *The Semantic Web-A Guide to the Future of XML, Web Services, and Knowledge Management,* authored by Michael C. Daconta, Leo J. Obrst, and Kevin T. Smith [16].

Further reading is recommended on the subject matter of ontology, particularly Chapter 8 from the above-referenced book. The chapter from the book gives an overview that is easy to understand.

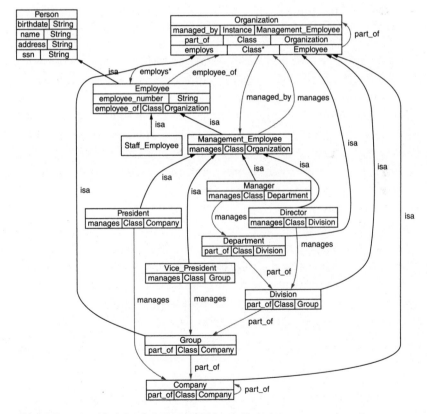

Figure 2.4 Graphical Ontology Example: Human Resources

Aside from all the technical descriptions of interest to the BI analyst, from raw data to a completed metric, the process is seamless in its execution and transparent to end users. And while it can be described as real-time business intelligence, in reality it should be metrics on-demand where anyone can get a snapshot of the current state on operations any time.

The current process is a reporting cycle involving many manual tasks to generate a set of metrics. That process is eliminated by automating the data mining and report generation through JMP. JMP data mining and automating reporting cycles have minimal to no impact on current systems since it draws from current disparate data silos. No changes are proposed to existing systems. People's jobs and roles will not be affected; rather their jobs should be enhanced if they use the metrics in support of their current roles and tasks.

By setting a standard competency in the production of metrics, redundancy can be eliminated as other organizations produce similar or duplicate reports. No single person or group is most or least impacted; rather the cumulative output of metrics should be thought of as the virtual business control room for driving and executing production across the entire enterprise.

The description of any particular JMP CONNECTIONS solution may be as comprehensive and complex as you want to make it since there is not much limiting you aside from time and money. If Level 3 maturity has been reached, the matured environment only opens opportunity for doing predictive analytics and further developing and managing knowledge assets in the context of the open semantic enterprise.

2.3 COST AND BENEFIT ANALYSIS

CONTROL COSTS—HUMAN ACHIEVEMENT—BENEFITS SYNONYMOUS WITH PROFITS

To paraphrase, the objective of this project is to facilitate our production goals. These include:

- More units to the supply chain and thus to our customers
- Less waste

■ Higher yields

■ Reduced cost per unit in support of higher margins

■ Taking competitive advantage to increase market share

The benefits associated with this solution include the following:

1. Increase utilization of data for running a more efficient business.
2. Improve the quality and accuracy of the data prior to analytics and reporting.
3. Reduce the number and use of spreadsheets.
4. Provide for an open system offering maximum flexibility when business needs change.
5. Scalable and incremental to meet new requirements.
6. Eliminate the cycle time currently required to generate dashboards, etc.
7. Optimize the delivery of metrics where and when they are needed and by whom.

The financial savings associated with this solution is a reduction in labor costs associated with elimination of manual preparation of metrics for dashboards, scorecards, and reports. The annual savings can be viewed as the elimination of one or more FTE units per year. A full-time employee's time is finite and cannot pro-offer scalability beyond a 40-hour work week without adding additional FTE resources.

The real cost/benefit derived from this solution is indirect in the sense that specific metrics supporting specific functional areas of production will increase the productivity of those areas and maintain a higher standard of performance due to the fact that better operational decisions can be made based on information that is near real time. So where do you measure the improvement? It is exactly here, because as a result of having implemented real-time metrics, the benefit is realized as a result of good baseline data previously unavailable.

The benefit provided is a method or knowledge engineering function to develop critical BI from raw data whereby the logic to produce the metric is captured in the codified SQL and is reusable for on-demand production of metrics. Great metrics allows for optimal human achievement to reach professional performance goals.

Maintaining the solution will be an administrative cost associated with keeping the micro-warehouse refreshed from the disparate data repositories. Recurring costs will be associated with JMP CONNEC-TIONS platform requirements to develop new metrics, or refining existing metric production entities, which are not necessarily new costs; rather they are part of the ecosystem.

In order to add some perspective regarding the costs, a project such as the JMP CONNECTION platform is to improve the capability and utilization of metrics for running a business and is incremental for achieving results. The level for this model is a bootstrap method for investing time, talent, and money whereby the more capability the results provide to the business, the more it makes sense to continue through to the optimal level. For example, automating equipment reliability by using control charts and predictive analytics in one organi-zation could conceivably go viral for monitoring all critical machinery across the manufacturing plant's entire operations, thus significantly improving business performance for the maintenance department. The reuse of codified logic and scripts within various departments in a business is another winning attribute that can be viewed as a dilution of the initial cost factors as a cerebral means of justification.

The only cost factor not addressed is the labor time required of the transitions (ie., from Level 0 to Level 1, from Level 1 to Level 2, and Level 2 to Level 3) capability. Part of the reason for not speaking to the cost factor is that we assume a portion, if eventually not all the FTE time, will transition as well. This text suggests the transitions take place incrementally and not as a major rollout, typical in most large IT/IS projects. Incremental development and usage makes more sense for small business and even departments within larger firms. Once arriving at the Level 2 capability, labor becomes a function of required mainte-nance on the platform and is a function of how much additional time is invested in developing new knowledge assets and metrics from the capabilities the JMP CONNECTIONS gives us.

The initial hardware costs associated with this solution (see Appendix E) and approximate software costs include the following:

1. X86_64 CPU—Approximately $5,500.00 inclusive memory, storage, graphics adapter, and display from Hewlett Packard depending on options ordered

2. JMP Pro: Please see https://www.jmp.com/en_us/software/buy-jmp.html#jmp-pro for details
3. Windows XP 64-bit license
4. Linux CentOs version 6 X86_64 Open Source

2.4 FINANCIAL ASSESSMENT

SIGNAL-TO-NOISE RATIO FOR MAKING THE CONNECTIONS

Before diving into an explanation about financial aspects, a little more must be discussed about the value of the micro-warehouse. The micro-warehouse is the heart of the DVS platform upon which investment in it and returns from it will be monitored and judged. One reason *micro-warehouse* was coined, was it actually came about from another context. A wide cross sector of the media world today is hyperventilating over the term *big data*[3] [8]. Big data is a big topic not because it is a lot of data, rather for what it is and why it matters. And, it is easy to imagine companies like Amazon, UPS, or Google using big data. In almost every way that people use BI analytics, one naturally goes from large data resources to what could be termed as *little data*. Now what one can learn from little data is that it is a new resource, a new raw material for the firm, a vital economic input that can be used to innovate. Once this mindset is realized, big data is also a vital economic input. The reason big data matters is we can now do new things with data that we could not do with smaller amounts. The topic of big data is for another book. For the JMP CONNECTIONS platform our focus is directed toward helping small and medium-size firms that are not likely to have big data, at least not yet; however, there are still lessons to learn from little data.

The micro-warehouse is derived through a value stream that depicts the metaphor of a funnel designed to filter out non-value-added data, allowing only the most valuable information to pour into the micro-warehouse container at the bottom of the funnel. The availability of little data drives this financial model. (See Figure 2.5.)

---

[3]Big data is a collection of data from traditional and digital sources inside and outside your company that represents a source for ongoing discovery and analysis [8].

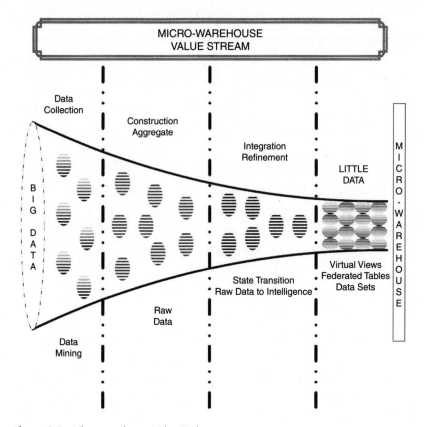

Figure 2.5 Micro-warehouse Value Tool

The majority of business men and women work with small data sets on a daily basis. Spreadsheets are the most common container for manipulating data. Needless to say, there comes a point in time in the life of a spreadsheet where it can outgrow its usefulness and is no longer an optimal tool. The sheet may become too large or a real software application replaces it. The sheer number of spreadsheets in use across the enterprise is proof enough that there is real power in little chunks of data. And more than anything else that is making the spreadsheet obsolete is the inability to do the real in-memory analytics. Thanks to JMP, features within JMP lends extensibility to a spreadsheet. Given the Federated Tables and Views, the micro-warehouse is the gateway or feedstock for business intelligence analysis whereby spreadsheets can go into the wide end of the funnel to be repurposed in the CONNECTIONS platform. Virtual Views created on a database server are well understood within the DBA community. Federated Tables on the other hand require a little more explanation. A Federated Table(s) on the JMP CONNECTIONS DVS is another novel way to access data that resides on a remote server. It gives the platform another window on data sets similar to a VIEW such that a particular data set of interest residing in a big data cloud somewhere can now be virtualized by keeping the data definition local on the CONNECTIONS platform without the limitations or restrictions of data replication. In other words, the data stays on the remote server and for our purposes we only want to look at it when our metric production platform demands it. In closing, Federated Tables are another method of data aggregation that can be configured and becomes a consolidated part of data integration on the platform. A more detailed look in Section 5.2 and Figure 5.2 helps to visualize this potential important piece that may be helpful to many when building out the platform.

This project to roll out a Business Intelligence Competency Center is not revenue producing in terms of cash flows and is not enabling for calculating return on investment (ROI) factors. Therefore, discounted cash flow analysis, payback, and net present value typically used in financial assessment have not been attempted. However, once real-time metrics have been deployed the normal aspects of the business where ROI is measured will see gains, cost reductions, and results that can be attributed back to the JMP CONNECTION model. The JMP CONNECTION model is a means to an end, not a sales product that generates a revenue stream. The end points enable the whole host of other activities that do contribute to profitable operations such as higher productivity, better human resource utilization, reduction of FTEs, and optimally better business decisions.

Eventually, the results from the project could be used to measure and demonstrate ROI. The JMP CONNECTIONS model itself does not have an ROI, although the model itself can be used as the measure of other improvement projects that are implemented. As a part of ongoing self-assessment, an organization has to be able to report and justify outcomes. So on the far end of completing the development of a particular metric one needs to be able to describe concretely such things as enabling the production of more marketable product. The cost reduction figures would factor into a calculation within the financial picture of the enterprise. Certain metrics contribute to cost avoidance within the enterprise because it enables making better use of your resources, too.

The cost of the working prototype, the sunk cost or a reasonable budget for hardware and initial deployment, equals approximately a $40,000 investment for the infrastructure. Financial assessment must take into account both tangible and intangible benefits. One needs to think about the financial assessment for each metric or set of metrics required for reporting a KPI as components of the JMP CONNECTIONS platform. For example, with the micro-warehouse already in existence, we may want to generate a metric for a critical piece of machinery for its reliability. To monitor a piece of equipment's reliability, a good estimate for developing the data management logic is to codify and script it in JMP. The intangible benefit we seek with monitoring this machine is world-class OEE performance that ultimately leads to a higher target average number of units or in other words more product to the market. The payback for developing this metric would be recoverable over the production life of the equipment or even by scheduled production campaigns. On the other hand and as depicted in Figure 2.6 on page 41, this implemented metric could be leveraged and replicated across many other critical pieces of equipment to monitor OEE. The OEE metric is an example of a reference to Section 4.2 on extensibility once a metric asset has been engineered.

Previously utilizing OEE on a more or less manual data gathering basis, the cycle time for getting an updated chart might be every two weeks. With the deployment of JMP CONNECTIONS, the equipment can be monitored daily with every batch produced simply by running the JMP script to generate a control chart. The payback for the financial analysis is less downtime, better throughput, less rework or scrap, and a higher quality product.

Other KPIs for inclusion into the dashboards would be similarly developed and assessed based on the assumption that the core micro-warehouse and JMP front-end are already in place. The more functional areas supported by metrics, the better the justification and payback there is for the project.

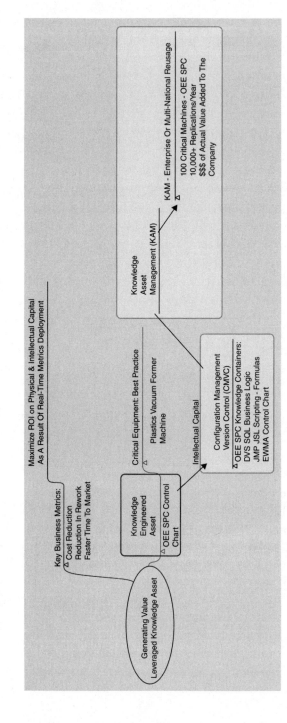

Figure 2.6 Generating Value—Leveraged Knowledge Asset

The financial assessment boils down to a firm's ability to take its data and filter out the noise through the funnel analogy. The signals from the data coming out the narrow end of the funnel are where the real value resides in making the connections, building the models, and maintaining a picture of what is really going on within the company. Complex economics within the firm are intractable problems due to the disconnects. Try coordinating a product line with the market conditions and marketing representatives in the field for optimizing sales results. Try matching up future work plans and labor utilization of the workforce. Assessment is a perceptual realization. The financial concreteness is most striking when the Data Virtualization Server is backed up and one is taken back by the smallness of its size in comparison to the volume of the big data that it came from. A second look is required just to make sure you can believe what your eyes are seeing. A large volume of high-quality metrics, reproducible on demand from little data, is truly leveraged innovation you can count on.

2.5 IMPLEMENTATION TIMELINE

The timeline for implementing this capability model depends on a number of variables. The implementation factor includes the type of priority given to conduct the changes required to migrate to a higher maturity level of metrics within the limits of your organization.

2.5.1 Contemplating Startup

Certain business settings vary in size and complexity as well as how production is structured (i.e., job, batch process, or flow production). Sometimes just getting started is an accomplishment. Typically, departments within an organization many times turn to their business analyst in the IT department with the idea that the IT group is going to provide a solution. Usually the onus is given back to the organization from the IT group requesting written requirements and specifications. And the reason for that is, unlike the early days of business data processing departments (i.e, 1970s), the data services had integrated within their departments subject matter experts working with systems analysts. The analysts actually worked on drafting tables to draw the flowcharts mapping the business process logic that eventually became a specification for writing the COBOL programs to run production. Most of the time these were batch computer jobs for generating everything from production work orders and customer invoices to printing paychecks. Today, IT departments play more of a support role and the larger enterprise projects get outsourced. As a result, the local data critical to the production floor or business processes many times does not reside as enterprise data. So, the IT group may not be aware of the data sets and how they are used.

As suggested earlier, starting a deployment on a small scale is fine for a small business or even a department within a large company for proof of concept. Of course another means of starting up an implementation mostly within a medium-to-large enterprise is getting the buy-in from upper management, particularly if it is going to be an ambitious project. The challenge with this concept is even though one gets the green light to go, the IT group may not have the personnel to execute the plans. Being an IT person does not make one into a BI analytics person. And neither does the term *data geek* really define what skills are required to do business intelligence work at exceptional levels. An attribute that sets one company apart from another, "competitive differentiation," is where BI makes a company more agile, better able to meet changing business needs and economic conditions. Business users are the consumers of BI. Those consumers exist all the way from a general high-level strategic position to the more granular levels at the production floor. In the larger aggregate picture of what a BI Competency Center should be, the BI implementation, which is what JMP CONNECTIONS is all about, serves to synergize organization(s) across the enterprise in a way that SOA (service-oriented architecture), mashups, and data management skills from data warehousing, OLAP, or data mart models cannot. The SOA, mashups, and OLAP-type technologies still have their place and may actually be inputs to a JMP CONNECTIONS platform; however, due to the nature of and original philosophy behind these technologies, they were not conceived in the way people think about and use BI in today's world.

2.5.2 Skills Dependencies and Timeline Consideration

A timeline for implementation should consider personnel resources and the skill sets available for the staff that will be working on the project. A discussion of what BI skills are appropriate for persons working in this arena may dictate the pace and perhaps the scope of planning and mapping out the implementation. This part of implementation is not as clear-cut as getting a certification from some third-party organization for various team players. Certificates look good on a resume. It does not mean one can do the job. And, it should be clear from the start that working in BI is something that does not fall in the "specialists" category. The most common career path people take in the IT field is to specialize in one skill area such as development or programming, managing software quality assurance and testing, and so on. The following is a list of career life skills that bring out the best BI workers:

1. Leadership, customer serving, and calculated risk taking
2. A business degree—Management Information Systems
3. Work experience within business organizations
4. Deep technical experience in the IT/IS realms
5. Deep knowledge about the business and infrastructure one is working in

This abbreviated list is very general for a reason. Hiring BI people is really about getting individuals with a lot of experience under their belt. That experience must be a diversified set of work/life skills across as many levels within a company and/or various types of companies as possible. Experience is reflective upon the fact that such individuals are self-motivated toward constant learning and acquiring new skills over the course of their career. It is not uncommon to find those who have done contract work in IT to be such individuals. Going from job to job, in order to remain competitive in the job market and get the best pay rates, those persons must continually maintain their technical skill levels at the cutting edge of newly introduced technologies to be marketable. Thus, they have honed their problem-solving skills unlike no others.

Experienced BI people must lead. And who are they leading? They are leading their customers, showing the vision and garnering more and more support. Collaboration is a key skill when face-to-face with company managers, business analysts, business users, and various IT disciplines to decide what analytics are appropriate, to show new knowledge discovery and how to use it in terms of actions that can be taken—identifying risks and qualifying and quantifying risk regarding the development of new metrics and whether the time and resource expended will add value to the products. For example, metrics that monitor waste through Lean Six Sigma or Process Analytical Technology (PAT), that drive to do things right the first time, can significantly drive down write-offs.

Any and all hands-on business experience is truly a skills requirement. Work in operations management, accounting, or statistical analysis is paramount because BI is more about running the business by the numbers, not guessing or gut feel. It is not about the journey or behavior necessarily. It is imperative that the mission and standard operating procedures are already in place. Metrics can measure certain aspects of behavior such as operator error nonconformance issues. Thus, metrics alert us to the occurrence of variation and outlier parameters within the context of the business environment.

Deep technical multidiscipline experience is a requirement to maximize successful implementation outcomes. Without the technical experience, problems can and usually do intimidate people too easily. Without the technical experience toolkit skills, it is more difficult to perceive and develop solutions to certain problems that seem almost intractable. An excellent example of this scenario and some practical experience would be to design a solution for a problem using and integrating open source software[4] resources. Open source applications and tools are typically developed entirely separately from one another. It is amazing to see how many different open source projects can execute as one coherent package where separately they were originally developed for entirely different reasons. The ability to create the architecture and structure toward a solution is comparable to JMP CONNECTIONS data aggregation and integration work leading

---

[4]See Open Source Initiative Definition, http://opensource.org/osd.

to the innovation in data discovery that was otherwise not feasible or possible under a Level 1 capability due to the manual labor involved. And unlike a regular rollout of a large IT application, BI may be constantly changing. Support for new data as well as new dashboards, scorecards, and reporting will push the requirements of BI projects. As BI implementations mature, customers begin asking for new metrics. The BI analyst with the experience can readily advise people about what metrics can add value and what requests may be superfluous.

Finally, once a BI person is hired or found in your company to help, that person may have to become embedded into your production or business organization for a couple of years to learn your part of the business if he or she is not able to work with subject matter experts. In any event, sometimes in larger organizations it requires time just to locate where all the data resides. In this section, the discussion strived to give some frame of reference for development timelines such that its dependency on skill sets should be factored into the planning.

2.5.3 Implementation Starting Point

Based upon the previous discussion about skills, it is assumed here that as a starting point, your organization is already doing some amount of metrics below the Level 2 capability, preferably at Level 1. As a practical matter, we also assume that the effort to graduate from Level 1 to Level 2 is not going to be an enterprisewide initiative. Just as previously stated, a JMP CONNECTION implementation is not a CAPEX scale project; it is a small-size task that if successful could go viral within your entire enterprise as other groups realize the gains made by the dynamics of producing metrics on-demand.

The implementation timeline is further determined by evaluating your current inventory of slides, dashboards, and reports that are in use. In choosing which metrics should be included, classifying them or putting them into a list of categories is very helpful. Metrics identified as providing for status reports that are representative of frequent extemporaneous events must be considered for conversion from a cycle-based method to an on-demand production outcome. Other reports such as a once-a-month safety report probably do not take up as much cycle time to generate and business users are not needing the information on a daily basis. Infrequent KPIs would be good candidates to put off conversion to a later date. Once classified, it should be determined which metrics are candidates for enhancements such as improved graphical presentations. Once you determine exactly the number of metrics that support the KPIs your customers require, estimates can be made regarding the time allocated to upgrade that piece to Level 2 and priorities assigned. As each metric is converted, the cycle time is reduced or eliminated altogether due to the fact that it no longer requires the BI analyst time to manually generate and publish the metric. Therefore, the previous cycle time that was consumed is now available to personnel to work on the balance of those metrics targeted for conversion that have been mapped into the implementation timeline.

If a customer's organization is coming into new or an upcoming production period, finding out if there are any new business requirements for KPIs can be evaluated and figured into the time-line equation. It is important to note, one would not implement a new requirement at the Level 1 capability and then do it again for Level 2. The capability levels described are not a structured means to an end. There is no savings, only additional expense if one were to incorporate a milestone Level 1 into the timeline for a new metric development because Level 2 capable metric is the optimal and ultimate goal. So as a structured means to an end, the capability levels of the model are not necessarily a stepping-stone process.

As a timeline example, assume a set of dashboard KPIs have been identified and agreed upon for implementation to include four KPI metric categories containing approximately six to ten slides for presentation. Thus, for a small project just starting out one FTE has been assigned to conduct the implementation for migrating this set to the Level 2 capability. It is estimated to take one business quarter for the development time assuming you have a skilled BI person working on the task. If the JMP Pro licensing and workstation hardware are not immediately available and configured, prototyping on lesser hardware such as a 32-bit workstation is an option. (See Figure 2.7.)

As one enters into the second quarter going forward, the JMP output of metrics will be checked for accuracy and end-user

Milestone	Task	Delivered Capability	Summary
Quarter 1	Upgrade Level 1 KPIs	KPIs @ Level 2 Maturity	Starting with KPI set at Level 1 upgrade through scripting and automation finishing out at Level 2 capability.
Quarter 2	Unit or System Test and User Acceptance Testing	Presentation and Delivery	Delivery as required by end users in the form of slides or Web browse-able online.
Quarter 3	Data Discovery & end user requested updates	Added refinements or annotations	Deliver enhancements enabling better decision making capability from KPI information.

Figure 2.7 KPI Development Timeline

acceptance. Accessibility, delivery, and presentation to your business users will be developed and refined as well. Ideally, in the next quarter there will be time available to deliver on the new nuances and annotation of metrics as a result of data discovery, hunches, and correlations. Keeping with simple timelines is appropriate for the small project to gain managerial experience in identifying realistic milestones.

JMP Pro may also decrease implementation timeline estimates. If JMP and JMP scripting is already being used at your Level 1 capability, those scripting resources do not necessarily need to be reinvented. They can be rolled into the on-demand platform to front-end such things as the database connectivity and structured query language statements that drive data into JMP tables. The primary purpose for utilizing JMP Pro as the hub of connectivity is no other statistical software tool exists in this form that supports in-memory analytics as well. Using JMP Pro adds to the importance of hiring an experienced person familiar with statistical software because sophistication of BI is more than just your spreadsheet graphics.

2.5.4 Implementation to Deployment

Implementation is the work it takes to develop the JMP CONNECTIONS platform, whereas deployment means your customers or user communities take delivery of the metrics made available by the platform for use in their everyday business activities. Deployment in the context of a competency center is where knowledge assets are centrally managed, with development and production of metrics, and more likely ownership of master data management for the enterprise hosted.

Experience is a prerequisite for digesting the technology specifications for use in developing JMP CONNECTION solutions for implementation work, especially as emerging technologies such as mobile BI, nonrelational databases, data retrieval from non-traditional data sources (i.e., point of sale (POS) terminals, instrumented devices like programmable logic controller (PLC), unstructured data from social networks, and so on), data correlation techniques, utilizing cloud computing, and on-premise and available data subscription services play an increasing role. An emerging technology often contributes toward decreasing the implementation timeline. For example, if one does not need to be concerned where the data is coming from in the cloud,[5] nor its configuration, through a simple Internet protocol, receipt of data as delivered to the DVS for use by JMP Pro scripts requires little or no implementation time. Then, perhaps all one is left with is to develop custom scripts for statistical analysis on the data sets coming from those abstracted cloud resources.

In this last discussion section, experience is critical to timely implementation and ultimately a deployment for your customer base. If the experience levels are more general and less in depth, expect the timeline to be longer in realizing implementation goals and delivered BI end product or services.

---

[5] *Cloud computing* is a marketing term for technologies that provide computation, software, data access, and storage services that do not require end-user knowledge of the physical location and configuration of the system that delivers the services.

2.6   CRITICAL ASSUMPTIONS AND RISK ASSESSMENT

2.6.1   Critical Assumptions

GOOD METRICS = ACTIONABLE INTELLIGENCE

The overriding assumption is the belief and high probability that just like improving upon a production or business process, improving the way we produce knowledge from a sea of data and executing upon that task will drive performance to ever higher levels. And, BI is in the unique position of gaining an exponential rate of growth and profitability for the firm because it has the opportunity to help multiple organizations and teams in an enterprise do better to optimize all their potentials for success. Otherwise, if that were not true, then people would stay with the status quo.

Within the overriding assumption, two critical assumptions should be noted.

> (A) Good metrics depend on the conversion of knowledge from subject matter experts into the business logic that transforms data into actionable intelligence.

> (B) Certain metrics once developed will continue to undergo refinement.

For example, at the capability Level 2 maturity, once mastering the production of control charting a piece of equipment for reliability and OEE monitoring, the next or third level (Level 3) of maturity is capturing data for predictive analytics in support of the Total Productive Maintenance (TPM) program and one of many reasons for deploying JMP Pro. The second assumption is ultimately leading toward achieving the third level of maturity, that once FTE hours have been freed up, leveraging the accomplishments of the Level 2 metrics in many areas will be a natural entry into predictive analytics, modeling, forecasting, and providing expert decision support to decision makers not previously available.

2.6.2 Risk Assessment

SCOPE, TIME, AND COST RISK FACTORS

Typical managed projects have risks associated with scope, time, and cost. Given that JMP CONNECTIONS is a model for a very small task with a certain number of steps known in regard to accomplishing the work, risk factors of scope, time, and cost may not be as important for initial conversion work. For example, taking one or two manually produced metrics from a Level 1 to a Level 2 capability may take one person two weeks to complete. This early phase work is an opportunity to learn what the scale of the risk factors may be for applicability toward expanding from a task-based approach into a larger project framework. Unless this initiative turns into a major enterprise objective, risk factorization may be less formal. Risk identification, analysis, and scoring conducted for big projects is more formal due in part to the amount of time and money invested.

However, a simplified qualitative BI risk factor (BRF) may be used in analysis and remediation of risk during the project. First, identify the risk. For example, risk with respect to personnel experience levels of those employed to oversee, develop, and implement the work can easily be shown in a tabular matrix. The template in Figure 2.8 can be used in qualitative risk analysis to score any identified risk in the project.

The BRF can be categorized as low, medium, or high. The conditions may be based on the experience levels of those involved. A person(s) or team with a high experience level will have a low impact when factoring a score. On the other hand, a person(s) or team that has a low experience level, for example, perhaps never having implemented and deployed metrics, may have a high impact to the project with respect to risk. The risk may be associated with the fact that it

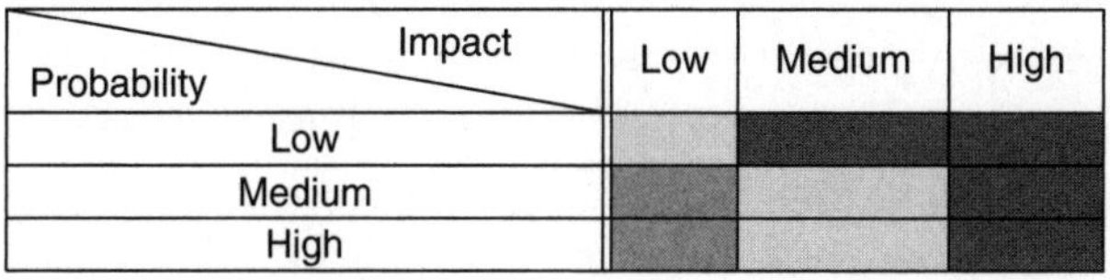

Probability \ Impact	Low	Medium	High
Low			
Medium			
High			

Figure 2.8   BRF Risk Assessment

may require more development time to execute the project plan when utilizing a team that is relatively new to BI projects.

The BRF Risk Assessment speaks more to qualitative risk than to quantitative risk because quantitative risk is easier to identify and resolve with contingency plans. An example of quantitative risk might be the failure rate of equipment. Therefore, a list of qualitative risk categories for consideration follows:

1. Quality of human resources
2. Quality of data
3. Quality of requirements
4. Quality of organizational processes
5. Quality of training
6. Quality of logistics
7. Quality of equipment
8. Quality of environment
9. Quality of decision making
10. Quality of software
11. Quality of IT processes
12. Quality of enterprise architectures

Obviously our focus on the risk factor for the quality of human resources with known skill sets is potentially of more concern and once assessed must be managed throughout the life of the task or project.

For each risk identified, a matrix template could be used for BRFs that are low, medium, or high and plug in a percentage for evaluation and scoring. A good resource for risk assessment and management plans with standard matrices for probability and impact are available from the Project Management Institute PM Body of Knowledge PMBOK Guide's *Book of Forms* companion guide [23].

Rather than having a risk response plan as applicable to larger projects, one only needs to be aware of competency limitations in this example. In the smaller initiatives, the quality of human resources issues may be partially remediated in circumstances where other teams or internal customers may have a resource that can overcome or resolve the potential BRFs. For example, the person working on the JMP CONNECTIONS may be very strong with programming skills and less experienced when it comes to statistics. The group that your BI work is supporting may have a statistician on-board that could implement a component part on your behalf, thus eliminating a risk factor associated with a lack of skill to complete a task. Proactive risk assessment is part of being innovative and creative where smaller projects tend to allow for creativity for resolving known risk factors.

Initiate *soft risk factors* versus *hard risk factors*:

1. Soft risk factors can be categorized as those factors that are not technical in nature.

   a. Over-promising and under-delivering on metrics. For some, this issue may not be a risk particularly if your scope of work in getting from a Level 1 to a Level 2 capability is not known to your user community. However, if your initiative is supporting a number of different groups, delivering a handful of in-actionable reports will not earn you much credit. To avoid this risk, early in the implementation service only one group at a time, establish and stick to a delivery schedule, and do not try to do it all at once for everybody.

   b. The value of a BI tool is not self-evident to nontechnical people. This risk has to do with "resistance to change." Avoiding this risk involves clearly communicating the usefulness of the project. Show added value, not added hassle. And, explain how the JMP CONNECTIONS assists them to complete their job more efficiently and to a higher standard. Do not fall into the mode of simply reporting and tracking activities. More importantly, a metric that melts away any opposition to change is one that reports on results. People realize its value when they can see comparative results from period to period, and marked improvements upon hitting targeted goals. And when a metric is illustrative of a problem or falling short of a goal, the results will aid the organization in building action plans to address issues preventing achievement. Thus, tracking results in subsequent periods will certainly show progress and in fact becomes a tool people can engage. As a result, this type of risk is no longer a factor.

c. <u>Poor adoption by your user community.</u> If no one uses the metrics, no matter how good they are, the potential benefits will never be realized. The following are some solutions to consider in avoiding this risk:

---

1. Include representatives from each defined user group in your customer base with the project delivery person(s)/team to allow input from end users throughout the development cycle.

---

2. Support the end-user community after the metrics become available.

---

3. Deliver iterative results that cater to business needs. Business needs must drive the technology, not the other way around.

---

4. If people are not using the metrics, ask them why.

---

5. You can also stop producing the metric and see if anyone complains. If not, then you never have to do it again.

---

2. Hard risk factors can be categorized as those factors that are technical problems.

a. <u>Business transformation, count on it!</u> Failing to account for change is a risk that is hard to anticipate. Planning is difficult because to facilitate change, technical factors do not always allow for a rapid transition. While this issue may be a collaborative and uncoordinated transversal among different areas of the company, business decisions cause these shifts. The technical problems, as a result of going from conceptual and perceived needs, will impact the work in progress on JMP Connection BI metrics. Creating the specifications and actually modifying the target KPIs and associated metrics in some cases seems like a combination of soft and hard categories of risk that must be dealt with.

Reporting needs, data models, and data sources will always be in a state of relative flux. In order to minimize this type of risk, each phase of development can be done in an iterative manner, continually ensuring that development is catered to the actual needs of the business. Given that the design and time-frame specification for conducting JMP CONNECTIONS is relatively short, change is less likely to occur over the shorter time spans as opposed to large projects that can run 12 to 24 months.

b. Hardware availability and compatibility circumstances. Another risk factor that may impede progress is lack of the right hardware being available where and when you actually need it. As a resource issue, sometimes workaround solutions can be put together until the ideal pieces come together. In so doing, the compatibility issues are secondarily complementary to what a hard risk factor might be. They are hard simply because overcoming them is not easy.

c. Quality of data is lacking. Quality of data refers to its fitness for use and is really a potential risk located at the data aggregation and integration stage for JMP CONNECTIONS. Making sure the data is clean, consistent, and not subject to frequent changes from your silo resources will prevent metrics that are meaningless or inaccurate. However, putting strict data change management processes in place to ensure that alterations to source systems do not accidentally, or unknowingly, affect the production of metrics may also bring about difficulties in developing adaptations for when the business environment and requirements change.

Building out the platform, the BI analyst has charge of minimizing risk during the period of deciding what siloed data resources can be aggregated either in the micro-warehouse or from the various other connectivity options available. For the sake of familiarity, take, for example, spreadsheet integration. When would a spreadsheet be included as an integration candidate and when would it be prudent to exclude it altogether? This question of course depends on what data it contains and whether business requirements must have its inclusion. Spreadsheets that act as nothing more than a place to hold data may be a candidate. The sheet that has no real design or added-in macro functionality would be a good candidate for virtualizing its data contents into the micro-warehouse with very little risk. However, users may need an alternative means or ability to input their data via a web page. Or, you allow the user community to continue using the sheet, and one would write a script to mine data from the sheet periodically to keep the micro-warehouse tables as current as possible.

Then, you have the mega- or super-size spreadsheet that already has functions programmed into it even perhaps across multiple worksheets. For example, you can see many such spreadsheets at Martindale's Calculators online (http://www.martindalecenter.com/Calculators.html).

Take for example the CoComposter.xls (http://compost.css.cornell.edu/CoComposter.xls) spreadsheet. The illustrated spreadsheet referred to in this hyperlink is a complex sheet that is actually a calculator. Thus, if you were in business as a farmer or producer of composted garden materials, as a analyst you would have to determine what risk is involved if converting or virtualizing the data from the sheet into a database and incorporating all the logic into SQL or formulas into JMP. It probably would not be a candidate for inclusion. It is well structured as a stand-alone application in a sense that is not suitable as a BI input resource. On the other hand, its output might be desirable to add BI value if it can be shown that in aggregating with other data it would contribute in either the analysis or production of other KPIs. (See Figure 2.9.)

A key indicator that might be helpful in deciding if a data resource is a candidate for aggregating is for the BI analyst to come to understand what business logic problem the spreadsheet solves. Logic problems are

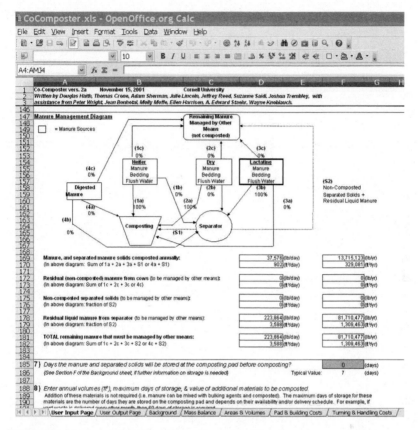

Figure 2.9 Example—Large Application Spreadsheet Type

finite and bounded. In Figure 2.9, it appears the problems it addresses are well structured and a great amount of time was invested by many people to build this tool. Consequently, the output may be the only thing that needs to be reported out and integrated into a dashboard format. Coming to this realization eliminates development risk and additional work.

Unfortunately, many spreadsheets are underdeveloped, and the business logic that is represented is fuzzy at best. They may be able to generate graphs and pie charts but the in-memory statistical analysis capability is obviously lacking. If a spreadsheet contains a large data set, the real potential knowledge contained therein is never realized until it can be treated like a table in a database. At that point, the relational power of the database engine can be leveraged by writing the query statements to draw out the key data subsets for direct use in JMP analytics.

2.7 RECOMMENDATIONS: TRANSMIGRATE THE ENTERPRISE

RETIRE THE SPREADSHEETS, ADVANCE TO JMP TABLES

Thinking holistically, the effort to build out the JMP CONNECTIONS platform, incorporating spreadsheets either into JMP tables or having them contained in the micro-warehouse, lowers the overall risk for the enterprise. One illustration of risk mitigation would be where applications, data, and database systems are required to be validated by federal regulatory authorities. Much has been written about whether a spreadsheet can be legitimately validated. Even though, for example, a company must comply with the predicate regulations put out by federal agencies, there can be much skepticism regarding the legitimacy of a validated spreadsheet. Unfortunately, modern spreadsheet design has yet to reach the necessary levels of sophistication for user control and data tracking as have other computerized applications such as databases and frankly requires supplemental technology solutions to bring them toward compliance. Regulatory inspectors[6] examine and audit for authenticity, data and system integrity, data confidentiality, and nonrepudiation. (See Figure 2.10.)

Regulatory inspectors also address the electronic spreadsheets' underlying supporting infrastructure and check that the proper qualification has been completed and documented. Thus, a primary recommendation is to consider the fact that JMP CONNECTIONS as well as the micro-warehouse can be in fact validated with a higher level of confidence for achieving regulatory compliance.

The question must be asked if fiduciary, reporting, and compliance obligations can be met, particularly in the case of a deviation event. Most corporate spreadsheets are not tested to the extent

---

[6] Since the 2002 Sarbanes-Oxley Act, concerns regarding spreadsheet usage for reporting and compliance not only in the financial services industry but for all public companies could and would be subject to inspections.

Document	Reference Source
Sarbanes-Oxley Act, 2002	http://www.sec.gov/rules/final/33-8238.htm
Data Protection Act, 1998	http://www.opsi.gov.uk/acts/acts1998/19980029.htm
Basel II: International Convergence of Capital Measurement and Capital Standards	http://www.bis.org/publ/bcbs118.htm

Figure 2.10 Financial Regulation Documents [13] [14]

necessary in support of meeting the fiduciary compliance. But what defines the word *most* in the previous statement without adequate data to back this up? It is nearly impossible to find statistics to answer this question, more than likely because businesses do not knowingly track this type of data. Large businesses may have a voluminous inventory of spreadsheets in use day-to-day, and a small subset of those are or should be validated for the appropriate regulatory authorities when decisions have to be made either by law or under license. However, there is another way to view the size of the fiduciary compliance problem and determine if it applies in the context of your business within your industry. Government agencies readily make available data on the citations, warning letters, or rule violations that are the outcomes of their inspection work. And from the government agency data, failure to validate computer software remains a persistent problem. The word *most* is an alert message here, but the inference made from an indirect examination of findings by agency inspections reminds us to be cognizant of conditions or inadequacies of fiduciary compliance. Uncontrolled and untested spreadsheet models pose significant business risks. Some of these risks include:

1. Problems and difficulties in demonstrating fiduciary and regulatory compliance
2. Potential loss of income/revenue and profits if found out of compliance
3. Poor decision making due to prevalent but undetected errors
4. Fraud due to malicious tampering with the data

Exactly why do these risk factors exist when it comes to spreadsheets? They exist because many spreadsheets are nothing more than "scratch pad" applications and it is generally recognized that errors can be found in a few percent of cells. In the large spreadsheet applications it is not a question of "if" an error exists; the issue is how many exist. Thus, some research is recommended in this area. Panko cites the following [28]:

> Despite this long-standing evidence, most corporations have paid little attention to the prospect of serious spreadsheet errors. However, in 2002, the U.S. Congress passed the Sarbanes-Oxley Act, which requires corporations to have well-controlled financial reporting systems. Even a single instance of a firm having a more-than-remote possibility of a material error or fraud in its financial reporting system will require management and independent auditors to give the firm an adverse opinion on its financial reporting system [27].

Formal testing in spreadsheet development is rare. As a result, serious errors may go undetected or may not be apparent. Some of the types of errors follow [20]:

1. Wrong inputs
2. Accidental logic
3. Wrong thinking
4. Accidentally overwriting a formula
5. Software surprises

For an exhaustive nomenclature in understanding errors, Aurigemma and Panko, "Taxonomy of Spreadsheet Errors," [9] is a good reference. Error mitigation techniques are useful for only certain types of errors. The error commission and detection rates inherent in spreadsheets in relation to risk levels may lead executives to conclude that an opportunity is available to achieve exceptional enterprise performance by initiating a "Y2K" type of error remediation program. Mitigation implies that a firm will implement tighter controls on spreadsheets because testing and remediation techniques for innocent errors are different than fraud-based errors where spreadsheets are used for financial reporting.

Building a JMP CONNECTIONS solution may be the ideal internal capital expenditure to remake the enterprise that substantiates a BI Competency Center to reevaluate assumptions and risks. The data validation opportunity is within the structured query language business logic and JMP scripting where exception reporting can go well beyond current-day confidence levels of spreadsheet validation.

CHAPTER 3

Technical Details and Practical Implementation

The technical details in this chapter may be skipped by the casual reader or persons not interested in thinking about the background or foundational basis of the JMP CONNECTIVITY solution. This section assumes the reader has a good grounding in the principles of information management systems or computer science with respect to systems analysis and design. The Harlan D. Mills Collection as hosted by the Tennessee Research and Creative Exchange (TRACE) at The University of Tennessee libraries at Knoxville are recommended reading and reference material for the software engineering student or professional practitioner. The expressiveness of Mills' work conceptually and mathematically for explaining or proving a design by his analysis techniques is truly complete.

The popular press and the wave of marketing typical in recent years promoting business intelligence solutions is almost incomprehensible. The flashy show-and-tell nature of dashboards and fashionable delivery systems yields little knowledge about how those items are generated. In the industry BI tools are known as dashboards, balanced scorecards, query and analysis, transformation, charting, data accessibility, and reporting. The front end sells; the details to generate metrics are just the magic that goes on backstage.

JMP CONNECTIVITY solution opens up the black box (BB) [21]. A black box is an external view of a system or subsystem that accepts stimuli. For each stimuli, it produces a response before accepting the next stimulus. In reality, assembling dashboards and the like deliverables is trivial. In fact, JMP scripting can be used to make your own customized presentation. Essentially a black box may represent a specific presentation metric but omits all the details of internal structure and operations and deals solely with behavior that is visible to the consumer of the metric. That is to say, what does the metric tell you and how do you act upon it? The actual computations required to generate a control chart as an example reside under the transparency of the black box.

One can think of JMP CONNECTIVITY or a metric contained therein more or less as a state machine (SM). A state machine[1] would be an intermediate system view that the BI analyst is most aware of. It defines the internal system state, namely the data store that may represent a process or performance data on a piece of equipment. Thus you could say that at this level it describes the black box by making the data visible.

The notion of a clear box (CB) is defined as describing the state machine. It is the system processing of the stimulus and state data. At the lowest level it may represent a standard operating procedure (SOP) whereby processing of which there are three control constructs—sequence, alternation, and iteration—that form the basis of systems from which we derive our metrics [21]. The SOP might state that upper and lower control limits are to be computed and that run rules are to be established for alerting when a process is either trending or out of control.

In an effort to give this discussion a framework and structure as well as some differentiation with other BI software in the marketplace, Figure 3.1 conceptualizes a high-level deployment view of the JMP CONNECTIONS platform.

The conceptual model of the JMP CONNECTIONS platform is a black box because it does not expose any details about the metrics. It is a state machine because it accepts the on-demand requests from the customer for a metric and produces a response or output prior to accepting the next response. The model is simply an abstract way of describing the behavior of the machine that has a certain state of being.

If you could open the black box and look at one metric, for example sales summary data, what you would see is a clear box that exposes the details for generating the metric. The data store may be the information from the spreadsheet. The state machine within the clear box may

---

[1] State machine definition can be found at http://www.techopedia.com/definition/16447/state-machine.

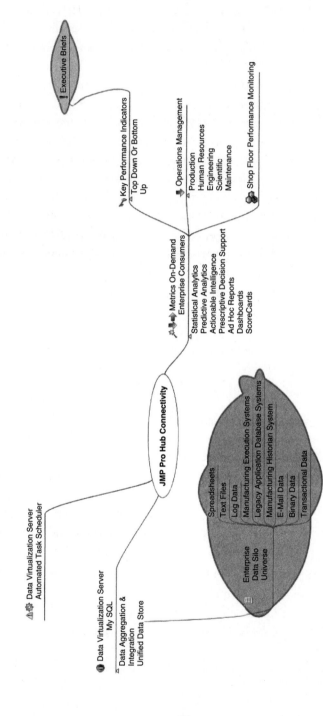

Figure 3.1 Conceptual Illustrations of the JMP CONNECTIVIIY Platform

contain a formula for trending the data and explains its various state transitions from the time the request is passed into it from the black box to the time it finishes and returns the metric back to the requester.

The understanding and construction of a metric, data, and control flow can be replaced by the three basic system structures nested over and over in a hierarchical system structure known as box structures. They essentially provide three views of the same information system or subsystems. The *hub connectivity* implies that customers are able to receive a wide inventory of metrics and KPI presentations. Collectively, the integration around JMP Pro makes this assembly of information possible. However, an individual metric represents a system or subsystem within an enterprise management information system. While there are many avenues feeding into the JMP CONNECTION hub, the main ingredient is still the many target metrics that support strategic goals.

As Mills, Linger, and Hevner state,

> Box structures were born out of the structured
> programming revolution, a paradigm shift that changed
> the way people were doing computer programming [21].

Trial-and-error computer programming came to be a software engineering discipline. And consequently a top-down development process allowed in a directed way the management of large projects. Ultimately, their work with box structured systems was the foundation for the Unified Modeling Language (UML), which became another development paradigm, an object-oriented approach for building large enterprise applications. It is easy to see how Mills' Box Description Language (BDL) and Box Description Graphics (BDG) led their students toward developing UML. So how could it be that these principles of analysis and design being taught at the university level enabled advanced thinking about development in the UML world? The answer is in the fact that structured programming has a mathematical foundation in the "structure theorem," which basically says that any flowchart can be designed as a structured program. Mills' methodology is grounded and derived from mathematical proofs.

Recommending the retirement of a spreadsheet and advancing to the use of JMP tables, in the process of modeling a metric such as a control chart, a metadata set can be defined with respect to data input, state machine, data reshaping, and output in the context of the box structured mindset. The same applies in the case when data input comes from a database rather than a JMP table. When a metric has gone through a robust modeling process and metadata accompanies the JMP script, firms can validate the scripts that produce the metrics when regulatory authorities require such compliance.

The purpose for introducing the box structured analysis and design methodology is to encourage a means and organized approach for developing new metrics that are not currently available. The platform allows for replicating the same metrics currently produced at the Level 1 capability. However, once the platform is deployed and the data integration and aggregation takes place, the more one works with the system, the more data discovery takes place and one can begin to see new opportunity. But from a financial standpoint, the organized method for design and implementing new metrics can gain buy-in from stakeholders because development can take place using the box structures of information systems methodology and thus can be completed consistently within schedules and budgets. Plus, it is a good way to document precisely the many system/subsystem views that a particular metric represents.

In addition, as stated above under the GENERAL CONTEXT, the implementation discussion will remain a non-CAPEX endeavor. So it follows that a UML development process would not scale, especially from a financial standpoint, but also because the intent is not to develop a large object-oriented application where UML is more appropriately utilized for software engineering projects such as air traffic control systems. Keeping it simple in all respects including a BDL and BDG model is a matter of practicality. It is easy to understand and reliable in terms of achieving that which drives the requirement to have a particular metric. JMP CONNECTIONS implementation within limited funding is not intended to start out as an enterprise-size project. Depending on the business environment, its place of development may be in a production area, sales and marketing, or even a finance department. Whatever the cost center, the premise is that as the platform becomes more healed, and it captures the attention of other managers and executives, through its extensibility it can become useful to other organizations in the business and end up permeating the enterprise.

As the BI analyst works through the analysis portion, it becomes evident at times that spreadsheets for instance, when originally created, followed no formal development process. Or, unstructured data, perhaps even data that is generated by a manufacturing execution system (MES) and historians, is nothing more than a dump of data. Using a good development process and methodology at the foundational and subsystem levels will result in adding optimal knowledge assets to the platform. In fact, BDG has a concurrent structure whereby its representation shows simultaneous execution of two systems and can thus handle complexity for a thorough mapping of system views. It is not uncommon to find concurrency of two systems or processes to be the case. When data has been integrated into the micro-warehouse where two tables contain information from separate processes, in order to produce the metric, a subset of data is required from both tables. These constructs as a result of the analysis phase then become an analysis library and useful in the design phase. The design library is a set of BDL designs where all of designs and constructs are the supporting documentation that describes a complete and precise box structure. The design documents are important for metrics that need to undergo validation.

3.1 HARDWARE FOUNDATIONS

HARDWARE CONSIDERATIONS AND SELECTION

The selection of hardware for the purposes of this JMP CONNECTIONS solution has a dependency on the software configuration as described in Sections 3.2 and 3.3. In short, a computer workstation must be a x86_64-based machine. The x86_64 is a vendor-neutral term and is an extension of the x86 instruction set. It supports vastly larger virtual and physical address spaces than are possible on older PC x86-based machines, thereby allowing programmers to conveniently work with much larger data sets. The x86_64 also provides 64-bit general-purpose registers and numerous other enhancements. As an example,

32 bits: maximum representable value $2^{32} - 1 = 4,294,967,295$

Storing an integer value larger than this value into a database on a 32-bit processor will return an overflow error because the factor that dictates these limits is the width of the registers in the CPU. Therefore, it is desirable to purchase a workstation that has 64-bit registers whereby the limit follows:

$$64 \text{ bits: maximum representable value}$$
$$2^{64} - 1 = 18{,}446{,}744{,}073{,}709{,}551{,}615$$

(the most common width for personal computers as of 2011)

3.2 SOLUTION STACK

SOFTWARE STACK

The solution stack is a set of software subsystems and components needed to deliver the JMP CONNECTIONS for producing business intelligence and metrics. Once the software stack is identified, hardware requirements can be ascertained that will become the platform to support the build-out of the objective. Recall that the whole reason for doing this is to be the competitive gorilla in our marketplace and survive difficult economic business conditions.

The JMP CONNECTIONS is a project that is not one that complies with the traditional software development life cycle (SDLC). The SDLC has a beginning and an end, typically managed on a project timeline basis. The SDLC model absolutely does not conform to the abstraction we call a business. A business is ongoing, dynamic, and constantly changing. Consequently, this platform is more or less a development laboratory that must be co-active within the functions of a business if the results are to be relevant and capable of staying abreast of changing business parameters. An SDLC software system once rolled out is like something that is hard coded and not easily amendable to change, which results in the system becoming obsolete over time. The BI analyst working within JMP CONNECTIONS software stack has the ability to not only produce consistent metrics, but also facilitate ad hoc requests and questions and experiment with new ideas where data can be turned into useful knowledge. Once JMP CONNECTIONS is built, it does not necessarily get turned over to an IT department or rolled into a data center. It is local to that business organization it strives to support whether that is production, marketing, maintenance, or distribution. SDLC projects are software engineering work; a BI metric is a knowledge asset, the production of which can be built on open source software stacks that of course have been derived from software engineering efforts.

The basic JMP CONNECTIONS software stack starts out with deploying what is commonly known as LAMP, which stands for Linux the operating system, Apache web server, MySql the database, and PHP the scripting language. For Windows the term is WAMP. Installing WAMP on a high-end workstation is recommended because JMP Pro will be running on Windows. WAMP stack distributions are readily available on the Internet and can be installed very quickly and commence running without advanced systems administrator skills. By default, Apache and MySql should run locally as localhost. In addition, the basic solution stack should include installing php-MyAdmin for database administration and development work and an ODBC driver for database connectivity operations. So as an example using your web browser, phpMyAdmin could be started as follows: http://localhost/phpmyadmin.

The same WAMP stack integration of software can also be deployed on a USB thumb drive and is entirely portable with the exception of JMP Pro, thus allowing for portability if required. This localized configuration is intended to enable the BI analyst to not only quickly develop a new metric, but also validate the business logic and continuous updating for on-demand use of a finished metric by stakeholders. In essence, the integrated use of the database administration, ODBC connections between MySql and JMP, and JMP scripting for a new metric is knowledge engineering and is the basis for turning raw data into a knowledge asset. Individual KPIs and metric reports do not require an SDLC mindset. The Metric Case Study in Section 3.5 illustrates the development of a metric that did not take a substantial amount of time to put together. The SDLC makes sense for large software projects that are finite in size and time.

Maintaining JMP CONNECTIONS as a core competency center for BI allows the business organization to continually improve the metrics year over year as time, money, and resources allow as well as factors such as optimizing opportunities or reductions in costs that drive the desire to see improvements. For example, going from simply monitoring a business process to forecasting or predictive capability can be a realized monetary incentive to become better.

3.3   INTEGRATION OF HARDWARE AND SOFTWARE INFRASTRUCTURE

FOUNDATION INTEGRATION OF HARDWARE/SOFTWARE

In Appendix E is a sample hardware requirement specification. The platform is robust in many ways. With 64-bit addressability quad core microprocessors, the memory requirement is essential for JMP Pro to handle very large tables for in-memory statistical analysis work. The hardware is capable of xVT for virtualization of host operating systems. With this option, consideration of a custom build out and system configuration is possible to optimize the use of the workstation.

In order to take advantage of virtualization, Windows 7 (Ultimate or Enterprise) could be the base operating system while hosting a Linux CentOs 5 distribution.

In addition, all other software installed should be 64-bit applications to run at maximum efficiency.

The stack is multipurpose and multitasking, not only for background tasks, but for hosting a database and network connectivity options and provisioned as a platform for delivering the metrics to target stakeholders.

3.4   BUILD OUT

ESTABLISHING THE ONLINE ENVIRONMENT AND PLATFORM PRESENCE

Building out the JMP CONNECTIONS platform can take many approaches and have varied configurations. The ultimate goal is to achieve an optimal installation that utilizes the real power available from the hardware.

Starting from the bare metal, thought should be given to the file system and its partitioning. Since hard disk storage is abundant at lower costs these days, 1 or 2 terabyte capacity drives makes this task somewhat easier since storage is no longer a major constraint within the system. Thus, for a system where virtual hosting will be deployed, installation of Windows 7 may be on its own partition. Another partition may be a SAMBA partition. SAMBA is the standard Windows interoperability suite of programs for Linux and Unix. A third partition may be reserved for virtual operating system hosting.

Windows 7 as a base operating system and a virtual hosted operating system such as Linux means that both are running simultaneously and of course are sharing the processor as well as other hardware without interfering with each other's operations. The SAMBA partition would be a shared file system between the operating systems.

On the Windows 7 side, all programs that are written for Windows such as JMP Pro would be installed. All other major software components from the stack which are mostly open source should run on Linux. Open source software includes Apache Web Server, and PHP Hypertext Preprocessor. These infrastructure components simply run and respond faster in an NIX environment than they do in Windows. The PHP (see Appendix A) may also be installed on Windows if scripts are run to import data into the database from Windows-based spreadsheets or data repositories.

Another reason for a preference to run a virtualized Linux OS is the fact that it provides a computing environment that provides a number of useful utilities and functions. A set of examples follows:

1. Cron batch jobs useful for maintaining current data in the micro_warehouse from data silos.
2. Version Control such as git or Subversion for maintaining control over programming code, JMP JSL scripts, PHP scripts, and SQL.
3. Utilizes less CPU resources than Windows.
4. Better security and reliability.
5. A platform for the delivery of metrics via web served pages.
6. A place to host data virtualization that results as the build matures.

A large part of the build out involves making the connections as depicted in Figure 1.2 on page 5. Therefore, initial testing must be done with all the potential connections. The transition from a manual process of producing metrics may require some development work. If data was being queried and exported from a third-party database application, a direct connection to JMP Pro with the associated SQL results should be confirmed or validated for correctness. Any connection to JMP Pro, possibly via a serial communications link, a streaming data protocol from a manufacturing execution system as from automation equipment, historian systems with web services interfaces, or direct access to a spreadsheet, all must be verified including the ODBC connection to the micro-warehouse.

Once the MySql database server is online, the micro-warehouse will need to be built out. The design and specification for the micro-warehouse is dependent on the number and sources of data silos that are to be aggregated and integrated. The build out is also driven by the type of metrics that are ultimately to be produced. These typically fall into the areas of productivity, cost, quality, and safety with associated KPIs for dashboards and scorecards. The build out includes writing SQL and JMP JSL scripts to codify the business logic. Coding of course facilitates continuous reuse for on-demand or cycle-based delivery of the metric.

A key element of a JMP JSL script with an SQL statement that corrals the data first into a JMP table is the ability to conduct the in-memory statistical analysis work by calling functions in JMP followed by the visual graphics that JMP can display. Anybody can open or create a JMP table, but in so many cases the time saved with a script is much more desirable than doing things manually from the JMP user interface and the JMP menu options available.

The following line of script is an example connection to the database with a query that returns a data set in the format of the JMP table.

```
dt = Open Database("DSN=Machine_Metrics;UID=jwubbel;PWD=          1
    sonora;SERVER=localhost;DATABASE=micro_data_warehouse;PORT
    =3306;",  "SELECT_sequential_cycle_number_AS_'OEE_Learning
    _Cycle', _stamp_press_run_time_AS_'Total_Run_Time' _FROM_
    oee_stamp_press_data", "OEE_HYDRAULIC_STAMP_PRESS_RUN_TIME
    _TRENDING");
```

When a graph is manually created in JMP Pro or any analysis for that matter, the script generated at run-time can be saved inside the JMP table for future reference or reuse. When actually writing a script, saving it inside the JMP table can be done in scripting as follows:

```
dt << New Script(                                                    1
            "\index{OEE_Run_Time_Trending}OEE_Run_Time_             2
            Trending_for_Hydraulic_Stamp_Press_Machine
            ",
Graph Builder(                                                       3
        Size( 1120, 735 ),                                           4
        Show Control Panel( 0 ),                                     5
        Variables( X( :sequential cycles ), Y( :Total Run           6
            Time ) ),
        Elements( Points( X, Y, Legend( 1 ) ), Smoother( X,         7
            Y, Legend( 2 ) ) ),.......
```

When the script is run, the code for the Graph Builder is automatically saved to the JMP table. Note the use of "New Script" directed at "dt," the handle to the data table.

In addition, in the same script the graphic can be automatically generated at script run-time as follows:

```
// automatically run and open the control chart so user does      1
    not have to do so
dt << Graph Builder(                                               2
        Size( 1120, 735 ),                                         3
        Show Control Panel( 0 ),                                   4
        Variables( X( :sequential cycles ), Y( :Total Run         5
            Time ) ),
        title("OEE_Run_Time_Trending"),                            6
        Elements( Points( X, Y, Legend( 1 ) ), Smoother( X,       7
            Y, Legend( 2 ) ) ),........
```

This last step is crucial to automate the production of the metric as it does not require JMP user intervention. From this point on, it must be decided where to save this metric for delivery to the customer or end user.

Once the metric is generated, there are a number of options to be considered during the build out with regard to delivery. JMP JSL scripting can do the following:

1. Send it to a printer.
2. E-mail it to a user or a group of users.
3. With JMP add-in(s) the metric can be saved to a Power-Point presentation or put into an Adobe PDF format or a word processing document.

4. The metric can be saved as a file to a file server.

5. JMP can generate html for serving it up in a web page.

There are two approaches for generating on-demand metrics. The question is, on whose demand do the metrics get generated? Allowing the end user to initiate the generation of the metric is one method. The other is confining the production to the JMP CONNECTIONS platform. Both have advantages and the basis for initiating a metric could be dictated by the type of metric itself. For example, real-time streaming data that is constantly updating a chart may be for the audience involved in monitoring a process. JMP JSL scripts could be made available to an end user so they can generate the metric they are interested in on their own schedule. If the user requires the option to generate the metric at a time of their choosing, the end user will need to have JMP Pro installed on their workstation. In larger firms the cost may not be as large an issue since site licensing is the norm. The advantage of end user–generated metrics also allows the end user to customize the metric with annotations or enhancements to the presentation format when appropriate.

By strictly keeping the production of metrics on the JMP CONNECTIONS platform, control is maintained over the JMP JSL scripts, and metrics can automatically refresh whenever new data becomes available or inserted, for example, in the micro data warehouse tables. Crontabs can be set up on schedules for checking for data updates and spawn the appropriate PHP script to update a table in the database. For data silos where it is known that data is constantly being updated or records added, a scheduled Cron or Daemon job could run during off–business hours and JMP would run the appropriate script to generate the metric. Scheduling task using Cron (http:// www.crontab.org/) comes from the Unix/Linux operating system environments where it is often handily used by system administrators. In Windows parlance, the Task Scheduler facilitates scheduling batch jobs or any JMP script on a regular basis. The Task Scheduler can be configured at the command line or its graphical user interface. The numbers of scenarios for automating the production of metrics are many. The principal scenarios include scripts written to read from data sources and refresh the virtual tables, batch files that automatically convert spreadsheets to csv file formats, scripts dedicated solely for the purpose of generating JMP tables, and JMP scripts for statistical analytics and discovery.

As the platform grows toward automating units of work, the Task Scheduler becomes a "third man factor" for the business. In other words you can think of the scheduler as your "virtual employee" because it performs directed work exactly when required. From a financial or FTE viewpoint, it becomes easier to estimate reductions in labor hours validating increases in productivity.

In the context of maintaining a BI Competency Center, keeping control over the programs and scripts assures that standardization is maintained and programming logic and formulas are changed only under controlled circumstances. To do this, code should be maintained under a version control system. The version control system allows for checking in scripts and checking them out for editing changes. Prior or older versions of the code can also be retrieved if necessary. The job of managing the business logic as captured in the scripts enables a degree of organization, when engineering changes to the scripts as a result of changes in logic or processes seem to be all too common occurrences. Retesting for quality assurance or for validation requirements will result in major savings, especially for the purposes of reusing code for incorporation into future applications.

There are various invocation methods available for spawning a process to generate a metric on JMP. Of course the most common way is for a JMP user to open a script and use the keyboard combination "Ctrl-R" to run the script. However, the main point of this platform description is to be able to set up and configure as much as possible the automation for unattended metrics generation. Other methods to spawn scripts include invocation from a disk operation system (DOS) command line. (See Figure 3.2.)

Figure 3.2 Disk Operating System (DOS) Command Prompt

The DOS prompt is the command processor or CMD.exe for the Windows operating system. From this prompt, the command to start JMP and automatically run a script could happen as follows:

C:\jmp.exe "graph_script.JSL"

If script files are passed to JMP on the command line, and a JSL file that has "//!" as the first line, it will automatically start running without waiting for user intervention. JMP table windows can also be made to be invisible so the script runs in the background.

One can also control JMP directly from VB or C#, which may be something that is provisioned for end user–initiated metrics generation. The programming is documented in JMP manuals and can be found by searching for keywords OLE automation. However, giving end users the means to generate metrics implies additional programming and development work just to give end users a control panel or dialog box for interfacing with a selection of options for the generation of on-demand KPIs.

Alternatively, installing Cygwin (http://www.cygwin.com/) on the Window system will facilitate better automation when it comes to running scripts. Cygwin is a collection of tools that provides a Linux look and feel environment for Windows. Where a DOS batch file may not be ideal, forking a process or configuring crontab in a Windows environment may enable the analyst to achieve the best results given the intent to automate the production of metrics. To reiterate, automating the process of generating a set of slides for a dashboard is what reduces or eliminates the aforementioned cycle time. Granted, it is assumed that the BI analyst should have some skills background in the Linux environment, in order to get the most work out of Windows using Cygwin. This little bit of effort is well worth it in the long run.

Finally, installing a great programmer's editor is almost next to imperative. Although JMP Pro user interface comes with a built-in editor for scripting, a suggestion to install and use a text editor known as Emacs is recommended for both Linux and Windows sides of the JMP CONNECTIONS platform for other programming and editing tasks that fall outside of the JMP environment. The following hyperlinks will direct you toward access and downloads of this free software.

1. http://www.gnu.org/software/emacs/windows/
2. http://www.gnu.org/software/emacs/

3. http://www.xemacs.org/

4. http://www.gnu.org/software/emacs/tour/

5. http://en.wikipedia.org/wiki/Emacs

Emacs requires some up-front learning curve to start, but once you get the hang of a few basic commands, a programmer probably will not go back to anything else. The real power comes in that it lets the editor or programmer keep their hands positioned on the keyboard most of the time, thus increasing efficiency for writing code. While it works on a desktop graphical user interface environment, many prefer the terminal mode. Whether writing a JMP JSL script, PHP scripting, or simply doing some documentation, text editing using Emacs will assure productivity remains high while concentrating on programming tasks. Later, one comes to appreciate the flexibility this old 1976 vintage editor is capable of when time is short.

3.5 THE CONSTRUCTION OF A METRIC

METRICS ON THE WAY TO A KEY PERFORMANCE INDICATOR

For many new to BI work, it may be a curious question about exactly how a new metric gets born into the organization and ultimately succeeds as a KPI. In many cases, this platform may simply redevelop existing metrics into a more refined product. Just when you think you have created the perfect dashboard load of metrics, someone else makes a request for a new metric and provides you with new requirements.

The first step is to take the requirement and define exactly what the requirement means and represents to the end user. This means that as the developer, an understanding of what the metric measures must be clear. The second step is to analyze or do some background research on where the data originates for aggregating it into the platform as well as any statistical calculations necessary to meet the requirement. At this point, it is feasible to generate a prototype deliverable with JMP. Once this step is completed, the metric can be presented to the end user to determine if it meets the user's requirement. The third step is the improvement actions where in most cases the user will suggest some refinements. The better the metric, the more effective it is as a control over the object it is intended to measure or monitor.

The steps outlined above may not always be a definitive way to work up a new metric; everyone may have their own process and time frame. A prototype may be a completely manual method to model it or in creating formulas that act on the data. When new strategic objectives or an enterprise initiative requiring a set of metrics for support is required and the stakeholders defined a new strategic objective or an enterprise initiative requiring a set of metrics for support and the stakeholders have signed off on the prototype metrics as the deliverable, the analyst can then start to write code for automating its execution and production of the metric for continued future use, reuse, or extensibility of the metric.

3.6 METRIC CASE STUDY

METRIC DEVELOPMENT BY CAPABILITY MATURITY REFERENCE MODEL

The case study is intended to show a practical approach, method of development, and the refinement process to a common metric used in an industrial application. The reader is reminded that in this single case referring back to Figure 1.3 on page 6, the JMP CONNECTIONS Capability Maturity Reference Model, a transition takes place from a Level 1 status to Level 2 by not merely being a percentage value to monitor, but a scripting outcome that provides an innovative control chart for statistical process monitoring of a piece of equipment. Second and more subtle is the transition from a Level 2 status to Level 3 by automating the script to run either periodically or on-demand. The improvement in efficiency justifies the investment because the automation reduces FTEs, and the script becomes a valuable asset for reuse on other critical equipment in the enterprise. At the Level 3 capability, the stage is set to conduct predictive analytics on machine component failures, which serves to eliminate costly downtime.

Given a manufacturing enterprise, a good case that is illustrative of a metric that has a good chance of being replicated across a production environment is *overall equipment effectiveness* (OEE). This case study is based on research by Fu-Kwun Wang, an associate professor in the Department of Industrial Management at National Taiwan University of Science and Technology as applied to total productive maintenance (TPM) programs [36].

A maintenance department is concerned with equipment reliability with respect to its availability, performance, and quality factors. TPM is a methodology for maximizing equipment effectiveness and over-all equipment effectiveness. Typically, departments may calculate OEE and graph this percentage over a production time period. And, that is about as sophisticated as it ever gets for evaluating the adoption of TPM in many firms. This case study will expand upon utilizing OEE data in a forecasting model of OEE with the ultimate goal of doing predictive analytics for reliability monitoring.

Assuming the example of this case study is our first attempt, choosing a critical piece of equipment to monitor is most purposeful when it shows or validates any benefits analysis component of the business case supporting the development of JMP CONNECTIONS metrics. Thus, evaluating and ranking exactly what equipment qualifies as critical is a first step. Examples might include a large sheet-metal press, air handlers that supply air to a number of sensitive produc-tion laboratories, or a specialized water system such as water for injection (WFI).

Overall equipment effectiveness data collected for availability, throughput, and quality are often gathered into a spreadsheet. Ideally, data input should be taken using a web form and subsequently stored directly into a database. Based on the infrastructure described in Sections 3.3 and 3.4, a simple web page using a JavaScript Object Notation (JSON), a lightweight data-interchange format, also works well with the server back end. A PHP script typically would calculate the OEE on-the-fly prior to executing the INSERT for the record. Alternatively, the data could be stored and a VIEW can be created that sets up the required columns for the JMP table import. A VIEW automatically stays updated as new OEE records are inserted into the database. JSON has excellent support in PHP. The web page is easily coded as an AJAX implementation, an acronym for Asynchronous JavaScript and XML. With AJAX, web applications can send data to, and retrieve data from, a server asynchronously (in the background) without interfering with the display and behavior of the existing page. The advantage of using the web form allows for data input validation either on the client side or on the server side to insure a greater degree of precision and avoidance of data entry errors.

With the availability of OEE data, this case study moves from a Level 1 capability where the percentages of OEE values can be used in a forecasting model, to Level 2, our next level of capability. The basic table of data necessary to reproduce Wang's work are %OEE, Estimated Errors. The errors calculated must be included in a JMP table. It is assumed here the reader has some familiarity with TPM. The concept of TPM is the enhancement of the overall effectiveness of factory equipment and the deployment of an optimal group organization such as a maintenance department for accomplishing system maintenance activities [36]. In order to build a forecasting method, *statistical process control* (SPC), which is traditionally used to monitor the stability of a process and detect variation or nonstable factors (out-of-control activities), is used to build a prediction model. As it turns out, Wang's work showed that by using a *time-constant learning curve* function to model, an OEE forecast can be treated as a process. Consequently, the OEE for a piece of equipment can be managed by SPC. The process control statistically, of course, is by means of a control chart and specifically, an exponentially weighted moving average (EWMA) chart. With JMP this exercise becomes trivial. The learning curve function is defined in Figure 3.3.

$$Y(t) = Y_c + Y_f(1 - e^{-(t/\tau)}) + \varepsilon,$$

where

$Y(t)$ = OEE (%) at time t,
Y_c = the initial level of OEE (%),
Y_f = the delivery data estimation,
Y_f/Y_c = the dynamic gain of OEE (%),
$Y_c + Y_f$ = the final level of OEE (%),
τ = the time constant (months) (a measure of how long it takes to achieve performance growth),
ε = the homoscedastical, serially noncorrelated error term with $E(\varepsilon) = 0$ and
$V(\varepsilon) = \sigma_\varepsilon^2$.

Figure 3.3 Definition of the Time-Constant Learning Curve Function

Thus, if a firm is adopting TPM, whether for one machine or for an entire inventory of critical equipment, management collectively can get a sense overall of a key performance indicator on the progress of adoption. The model using the time-constant learning curve is used to monitor equipment and easily foresee any instability. So at a high level, the approach compares the OEE with the expected values, and the forecasting process can be continuously updated. As Wang states:

> The deviation (forecasting errors) provides prompt
> information to initiate any necessary managerial actions.
> Using this approach, it is possible to improve the
> maintenance policy and monitor the process TPM [36].

The theoretical math is well covered by Wang's journal article. Understanding its application, though, is critical for success. When talking about deviation or forecasting errors, Wang's application of a learning curve model is equivalent to what one would see on a control chart when a data point exceeds the upper or lower control limits. A data point that exceeds a control limit would be an indication that something happened to the TPM program. Consequently, maintenance department personnel must be alerted so that appropriate action can be taken. The abstraction of a learning curve that shows any variation in our machine performance as a process must have assignable causes such as unskilled workers, parts wearing out, infrequent preventative maintenance, and other factors. The idea that learning is cyclical and therefore must be associated with a learning rate is profound. For example, take a machine that stamps out automobile car doors from 6:00 AM until 4:30 PM every day. If an adjustment is made to the machine, naturally one would want to learn whether that adjustment improves the performance of the machine. The machine's production is the analogue to a learning cycle. Another day's batch of doors is run. The OEE is calculated for that day's batch of doors. Each day something is learned, and this period is a cycle or opportunity for making improvements. If the forecasting errors start trending out of control, one may learn that the adjustment only decreased the machine's performance. Achieving an 85% OEE may mean that setup mechanics and engineers need to fine-tune the machine in order

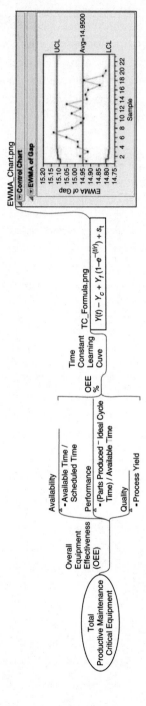

Figure 3.4 Total Productive Maintenance Conceptual Diagram

to achieve and maintain optimal performance and output. At each period, the machine may be adjusted, a component changed out, or a software program altered; then the control chart can be examined to determine whether the action taken improved the process (i.e., the performance of the machine). Sometimes changes need to be backed out because the learning cycle allows us to see what works and what does not.

Conceptually, the mind map in Figure 3.4 illustrates a model for statistical process control of critical equipment.

The following steps demonstrate how to implement the learning curve function to produce control charts for monitoring a TPM program as it may apply to a piece of equipment:

1. Collect data for each cycle and compute the OEE for that period (Figure 3.5).

Note that the data collected is in a consecutive sequence by day. In JMP this data could be a column of "value ordered" or sorted dates. In any case each day represents one cycle.

2. Next, create a new column in the JMP table for experimenting purposes (name it x-formula). The time-constant learning

	Day	OEE
1	1	59.8
2	2	64
3	3	64.5
4	4	60.2
5	5	64.7
6	6	59
7	7	64.6
8	8	61.1
9	9	63.5
10	10	61.6

Figure 3.5 Sequence Column and OEE Values Column in a JMP Table

function requires the specification of three parameters in order for it to execute. The new column is used to estimate these parameters using the Gauss-Newton iteration method facilitated by JMP.

3. Prerequisite to Step 2 above, Wang arrived at starting values by using a Taylor series expansion, which was used for nonlinear regression and is the linearization of the non-linear function. Wang's starting values were $[\theta_{10}, \theta_{20}, \theta_{30}] = [\gamma_{c0}, \gamma_{f0}, \tau_0] = [57.6, 10, 20]$.

4. In the JMP table, right-click on the heading labeled x-formula and select "Column Info." At this point the time-constant learning curve formula is input into JMP using the starting values of 57.6, 10, and 20 as shown in Figure 3.6.

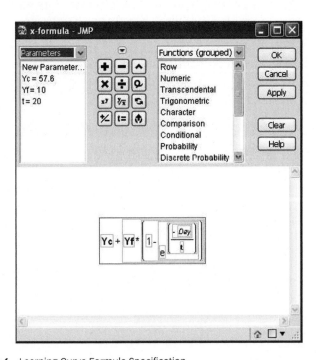

Figure 3.6   Learning Curve Formula Specification

The result of entering in the formula gives a column of data under the x-formula column in the JMP table.

5. The next step is crucial because the Gauss-Newton iteration generates the starting values needed for the learning curve function, which will give us the "Estimated OEE" data column. On the JMP menu, go to Analyse, Modeling and select Non-linear (Figure 3.7).

Use the predictor formula specified in column x-formula with the Y, Response set to the OEE column. Click OK. (See Figure 3.8.)

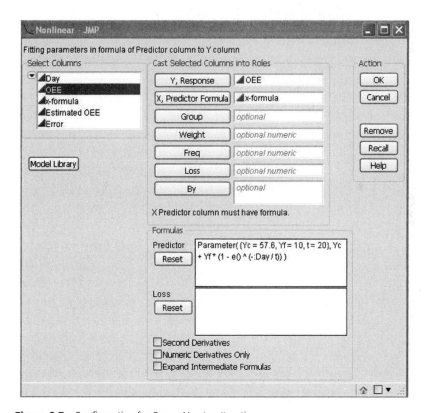

Figure 3.7 Configuration for Gauss-Newton Iteration

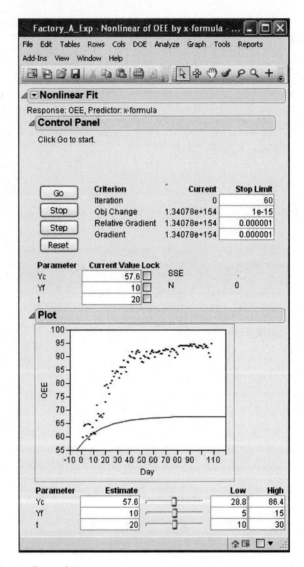

Figure 3.8 Nonlinear Fit Program

Notice to confirm the Response is OEE, the Predictor is x-formula and the starting values are 57.6, 10, and 20. (See Figure 3.9.)

The objective function (i.e., the time-constant learning curve in x-formula) was converged at the 11th iteration. The results are found in Figure 3.10.

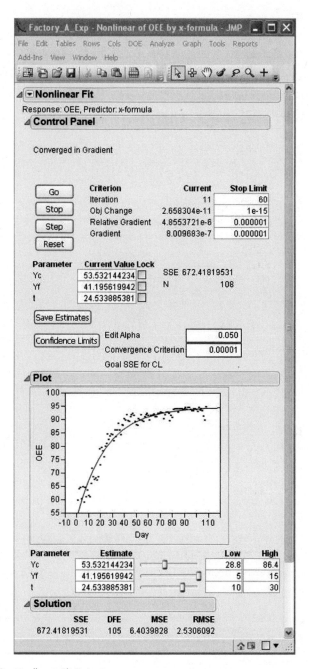

Figure 3.9 Nonlinear Fit Output

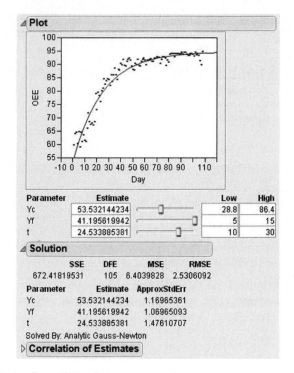

Figure 3.10   Nonlinear Fit Results

The results show a corresponding mean square error (MSE) = 6.403 and a root mean square error (RMSE) = 2.5306. The solid line in the graph is the time-constant learning curve for the data from Factory A. The values computed will be plugged into the learning curve formula for estimating OEE. (See Figure 3.11.)

6. Create a new column in the JMP table called "Estimated OEE." The time-constant learning curve formula is input into JMP using the values of 53.5319, 41.1957, and 24.5335 as in Figure 3.12.

$$\hat{Y}(t) = 53.5319 + 41.1957 \times (1 - e^{-t/24.5335})$$

Figure 3.11   Learning Curve Formula for Estimating OEE

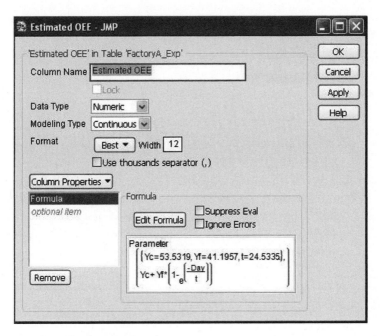

Figure 3.12 Estimating OEE Formula

Clicking OK to exit the properties dialog box for "Estimated OEE," the column computes the estimated values for each learning cycle.

7. Finally, create another column in JMP labeled "Errors." Select the "Column Info" to access properties and configure another formula that computes the errors for each cycle. The formula is "OEE" − "Estimated OEE." The errors are charted such that for those found to be out of criteria, that is, located outside the lower control limit (LCL) or the upper control limit (UCL), necessary actions should be taken during these periods that includes investigating and remediating the identified assigned causes for the variations.

8. The data in the JMP table is ready for generating the control chart. On the JMP menu, select Graph, Control Chart and EWMA. The EWMA setup and the control chart appear in Figures 3.13 and 3.14.

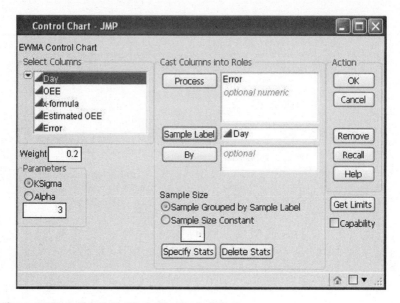

Figure 3.13 Setting Up to Display the Control Chart

Wang states the following:

> The EWMA control chart is very effective against small process shifts. The goal of monitoring changes adversely affecting the TPM's effectiveness is to activate a change process as early as possible. Ideally, the quality control procedure should activate a process before the data can be visualized as a change in the underlying rates [36].

Given the fact that our machine is stamping out car doors on a batch-per-day basis, it is preferable to monitor OEE daily rather than, say, every two weeks. Thus, the above steps would utilize a JMP script that replicates the manual actions described above so the control chart can be generated on demand assuming the information in the database is current. If new OEE data is added to the database for each cycle, the Gauss-Newton iteration must be repeated to get new starting values. Rerunning the Gauss-Newton iteration is easily accomplished in JMP JSL scripting as seen in the sample code in Appendix B. At this point, the metrics have reached a Level 2 capability from the perspective of our JMP CONNECTIONS point of view. The charts can become

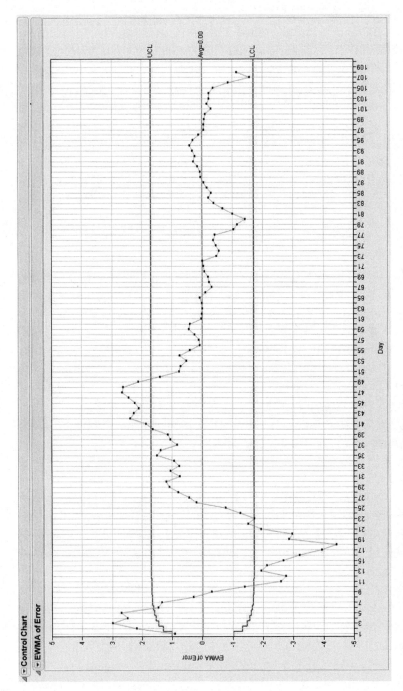

Figure 3.14 Control Chart with Forecasting Errors Out of Criteria

very useful for such things as comparing equipment performance of multiple identical machines. Typically, for many charted pieces of equipment, the maintenance department will find that improvements can be made in the early stages. Through empirical experience and a track record of using this methodology, the maintenance department may find that it has fine-tuned the machine, its OEE percentage is very good, but all of a sudden the charting shows a trend toward going out of control. One soon finds out that external factors are impacting the OEE. For example, let us say we are making hard disk drives for personal computers in a clean room. The HVAC or air handler for the room is going on- and offline, resulting in disruptions for work being done in the room. It quickly becomes evident that the air handler is another critical piece of equipment that also needs to be rolled into the TPM program.

So the question is, where do you go from here? Before considering the Level 3 capability, success at the Level 2 capability must be realized. Consideration includes such things as a reduction in cost factors associated with a machine's reliability and performance, more output due to less unplanned downtime, and noting if other departments are rolling this model out in their own production areas. All critical equipment has been identified and is currently being monitored so that one can say maturity has been reached with the Level 2 capability.

The fact that JMP Pro connectivity can be so pervasive means access to more data is important for using other JMP Pro advanced features like the predictive analytics. Engaging predictive models to determine things like when is the best time to do preventative maintenance and what is included when the maintenance is conducted requires more data for analysis. This data comes from manufacturing execution systems (MES) automation equipment in the factory and historian programs. Granularity of information about MTBF data on servo motors or other components on a machine subject to wear and tear become factors.

Embarking on the quest to achieve a Level 3 capability with the metrics when it comes to reliability also demands a requirement. This approach may be new or a change in our thinking with regard to the linkage between reducing our electrical energy consumption onsite and reliability. If management sets a new objective to reduce and conserve energy consumption, then the requirement definitely gives us a new consideration. If the focus has been on reliability, a new parallel opportunity also achieves savings by optimizing kilowatt usage or reducing our demand, resulting in lowering our utilities expenses. The primary reason we buy electricity is that it does work for us. A manufacturing operation spends for electricity on motor-driven systems, the cost of which is associated to pumps, fans and blowers, and air compressor systems. The plant transfers around a lot of fluids.

In many cases one may suspect that the motor-driven equipment operates with a notably lower efficiency than it could, which has an increasing effect on the motor-driven energy consumption.

Besides the energy costs, the inefficient operation of the motor-driven device may also affect the motor system reliability, since the mechanical reliability of a motor system is linked to the efficiency of the motor's operation, and a motor failure can cause notable additional costs as a result of the production losses. Consequently, the energy-efficient operation of a motor-driven system is often the key factor also to lower motor life-cycle costs (LCC).

At the Level 2 capability the focus is a holistic system view. So the interface between one machine to the next critical system could be a pump. Consequently, to monitor OEE in equipment upstream or downstream of a critical machine as the next critical system, we might start by doing the following:

1. Inventory the number and type of motors in the room integral to the production system.

2. Determine if the motors meet the minimum efficiency standards as set by the Energy Policy Act of 1992 (1 to 200 horse power) or National Electrical Manufacturers Association (NEMA) standards.

3. Review whether the motor is insufficient, sufficient, or over-powered for its intended application.

4. Make sure policies are in place for determining whether a motor upon breakdown is upgraded, rewound, or replaced like for like.

5. Look for system improvement opportunities that may include: improved sizing and proper matching to load, use of more efficient drive trains, improved system layout, updated and

well-maintained controls, improved operation and maintenance, and use of adjustable speed drives (ASDs). The system's approach collectively examining all motor-driven components contributes toward total OEE system performance.

6. Possibly most important consideration is whether a speed control method instead of the throttle or by-pass control method would lead to both higher reliability and lower electric consumption.

7. Determine if the following online software tools would be useful: http://www1.eere.energy.gov/industry/bestpractices/software_motormaster.html.

Thus, a function of our OEE availability and uptime is a higher level of reliability available from our power-consuming equipment.

These larger systems usually have larger power requirements. The type of motor is important as well. A centrifuge or large water pump is more likely to have an inductive motor, which is a brushless type due to the higher rpm requirements. As perhaps a not-so-uncommon example, a series of water pumps for circulating hot and cold water circuits are centrifugal pumps driven by induction motors. These are probably not variable speed drives (VSDs); the flow into the pump is throttled by a valve on the output side of the pump, not an optimal method of control. These pumps could be retrofitted with a frequency converter controller, thereby giving us the means to manage the efficiency of the pump by electronically controlling the rotation speed, resulting in lower power consumption. The frequency converter also gives us a sensor-less means to monitor the motor by estimating the rotational speed, torque on the shaft, and pump flow rates. The literature and research also says that a frequency converter can be used to detect cavitation and flow recirculation that contributes to wear and tear as well as using more electricity from resistance within the pump as a result of cavitation/recirculation. Optimal operating regions and pump operating point locations can be graphed such that one would know if it is running at optimal energy-efficiency and reliability.

If there are already frequency converter controllers on the induction motors, these could be a data source for making sure this equipment is OEE monitoring ready and yielding a means of statistical predictability for PMs before a crucial failure happens. For a single pump system, the savings potential in the energy consumption can be in the range of 5–50%, if a fixed-speed pumping system is retrofitted with a frequency converter.

Going to a Level 3 capability with JMP CONNECTIONS is necessarily more work, but the payoff can be substantial.

For additional supporting documentation, reference article "Learning Curve Analysis in Total Productive Maintenance." [37]

```
SELECT dayofyear(die_cut_date) AS Day, die_cut_date AS Date,
    lot_number AS Batch, oee_percentage*100 AS OEE from
    die_cut_data WHERE stamp_machine_location = 'Plant_29';
```
[1]

CHAPTER **4**

Harvesting Benefits and Extensibility

A unique aspect about working with BI data is that often subtle opportunities arise yielding benefits. Harvesting those benefits collectively across the enterprise raises a firm's competitive advantages.

4.1 BENEFITS EXAMPLE

OPPORTUNITIES LEAD TO BENEFITS

Taking the case study in Chapter 3 as an example, over the course of monitoring the car door stamping machine's performance and reliability for three months, fine-tuning and making adjustments, it was found that the OEE was still short of its goal, yet did not exceed control limits on the control chart. Meeting with engineers and operators and discovering assigned causes for investigation such as external factors impacting the line allows for attaining a resolution to the problem. The run-time known as end time subtracted from the start time was graphed, indicating the variation above the specified best practice time for each day's production cycle. To put the variance into perspective for management, the excess hours over the course of three months was equated to full-time equivalents (FTEs). If the machinery required 25 machine operators in the room, the extended run-time hours were due to factors such as upstream or downstream production holdups, or glitches taking place in the production room with the machine. Based on empirical work study, there was a total of one FTE spent on over run-time every six months. If an FTE is equal to 210 work days per year or 1,680 labor hours, and you have 25 people on the line, based on three months of data one can project 6 or 12 months' worth of FTEs times 25 people. It is therefore imperative to find out how to reduce this overhead.

The simple thing to do at this point is to go ask the operators. The solution to the problem for this example was the lack of qualified and skilled machine setup mechanics. Preparing the equipment prior to the start of production immediately improved operational performance, allowing the team to finish on time within the target best practice criteria. So the solution was to redeploy personnel with the right skills, resulting in less overtime, better employee morale, and a savings factor in FTEs because fewer people were required to get the job done. The point was not to eliminate jobs but to redeploy operators to other production areas to leverage their time and skills for gains in strategic advantage.

4.2 EXTENSIBILITY

EXTENSIBILITY LEADS TO RESILIENCE

A BI metric such as the OEE example can be extended across an enterprise. Two examples come to mind. Perhaps there are identical production machines running side by side stamping out parts. But for some reason they do not perform the same day to day. Using the control chart monitoring on both machines and comparing the performance characteristics will aid in the analysis to determine the factors that may explain the differences in performance. Differences might be particularly true when maintenance replaces a set of worn-out parts such as retractor springs that were not like for like. Maybe the springs were a softer compression rating. If the springs were not working properly 100% of the time, the variance would immediately start showing up in the control charts. The good machine might start taking up the slack from the machine that is performing less than optimal, causing a longer run-time on the good machine. However, the benefit of this extensibility is in having this situational awareness, being able to explain the cause of variation, and making the right business decision to order the correct part or even lose a day's production to have maintenance change out the parts.

The BI metric is often extensible because in so many situations, its applicability can be replicated. For example, if a large company is set up with many focus factories, the metric for safety developed for one focus factory can be also used for all the other focus factories in representing the data for total recordable injuries, first aids, and near misses. The United States Department of Labor and the Bureau of Labor Statistics (http://www.bls.gov/iif/) is the primary reference for computing total recordable injury rates.

Extensible also means that the platform can be utilized by many other business departments within the enterprise. It also means that other workstations will only need JMP on their workstations, not the entire platform as specified in this document. JMP deployment to workstations is critical and more important if users want to interact with metrics as opposed to static views or presentations. A script such as the one developed for OEE control charts can be made available, and the only thing the other group of users would need is to supply their own OEE data for each piece of equipment they want to monitor.

4.3 CONFIGURATION MANAGEMENT VERSION CONTROL

CONTROL OVER SCRIPTS AND CODE RESOURCES

Configuration Management Version Control (CMVC) may be a real possibility, a matter of practicality as a result of extensibility. For success not only with your enterprise metrics, but when others start adopting your work, there comes a time when controlling and managing the source code becomes a necessity. Once again, your source code is the inventory of JMP scripts, SQL, PHP scripts, or any documentation that supports the platform.

CMVC really describes a software product under development such as a word processing program, a smart phone applet, or a knowledge asset that results in KPI metric(s). Given that most software today is nontrivial, its configuration can be very complex. This complexity is innate from source code, build environments, and parameters, to multiple developers collaborating during the engineering, coding, and quality control phases. So it follows that managing these resources optimally can make or break a project as well as the software product. The key concept is of course version control of the soft assets, primarily the source code. Implementing a version control system promotes the *management* component in the term *CMVC*.

In the world of controlling versions of software, there are three archetypes or models. These include the local version control, centralized version control systems, and distributed version control systems.

The most basic way people conduct version control is on their local computer system or network. Creating or tracking versions is usually a manual process of keeping folders and file names with various naming conventions. The manual version system is very error prone and does not scale well for larger projects. The early centralized version control systems were applications that utilize database technology to track files and changes. The only drawback to these systems is they were not the best tools for collaborative development work.

For our purposes in managing the JMP CONNECTION code base, the distributed version control system that has enjoyed wide use in the software community is GIT. As per the GIT website:

> GIT is a free and open source distributed version control system designed to handle everything from small to very large projects with speed and efficiency.
>
> GIT is easy to learn and has a tiny footprint with lightning fast performance. It outclasses SCM tools like Subversion, CVS, Perforce, and ClearCase with features like cheap local branching, convenient staging areas, and multiple workflows [3].

The distributed version control system (DVCS) enables large or small groups of developers to collaborate and share code resources without bumping heads so to speak. If you are the sole developer in your company, GIT is a great tool for creating and managing a stand-alone repository. Over time, the repository can be shared or it can become a master repository on a GIT server where others can retrieve the source code, improve it, and merge changes back into the code base. Reaching the third capability maturity level where cycle times have been reduced and work on predictive analytic projects can go forward, a version control system will likely be a critical factor that firmly establishes the achievement of the Level 3 capability within the firm for the production of metrics.

GIT does not manage the resources that are added to the repository as file names. Instead, the files are treated abstractly as objects. In order to accomplish this, globally unique identifiers (GUIDs) are used and assigned to each "commit" transaction. The actual content is termed a BLOB or binary large object. Files that are changed and frequently committed back into the version control system can be retrieved from its earliest incarnation, all the way up to the latest or so-called head. A history is maintained and the change or delta(s), that is, the differences, can always be referenced.

Development cycle time is reduced because a DVCS facilitates code reuse. For example, a small subset number of scripts are found to be useful in another project. Consequently, the term *branch* is used to indicate that code identified for use in another project is forked, which conceptually is another development path, a new product, or metric for the platform.

From the perspective of the developer, and in the case of the JMP CONNECTION environment where data is aggregated from multiple silos, data resources like spreadsheets can also be put under control. As discussed previously, spreadsheets cannot be validated. And, if JMP executes scripts against the spreadsheet or data that has come from a spreadsheet, what typically can happen is someone decides to change the spreadsheet. A column was added or taken away and no one bothered to inform the BI analyst of that fact until the script executes and fails. Putting the spreadsheet into the DVCS is really for the purpose of maintaining or monitoring it for structural changes. Realize that the data in the sheet may constantly change, but within the control system the analyst or administrator can do what is called a "diff" operation and generate a log of what the differences are between two spreadsheets and immediately discern the problem.

Most of the metrics that are KPIs for business intelligence are non–GMP (aka, non–Good Manufacturing Practice) metrics. In other words they are not required to be validated. For example, in the pharmaceutical business, some process monitoring data would be considered by the FDA to be cGMP metrics, that is, process analytical technology (PAT)[1] and thus must have gone through a validation process. Validated data would be the case, for example, on automation equipment and process design, scaleup, and eventual validation and

---

[1] Many vendors, subcontract companies, or contract research organizations (CROs) provide support services to the pharmaceutical industry and have available Technical Briefs on PAT. See Particle Science Drug Development Services [30].

licensing. In these cases, formalized processes must be followed, known as change control management. If a change is something more than a simple administrative change in a document, that change must require validation or the equipment must also be revalidated. By placing software source code into a DVCS, it expedites and supports an organization's formal change control process for engineering changes such that the expectation levels for quality control over changes to cGMP source code can be met when validated. Traceability, tracking, and audit trails are key factors to satisfy federal agency for any industry requirements.

From minimalistic requirements to extreme cases, implementing version control sooner rather than later can be a legitimizing force for the BI analyst. Thus, when executing scripts for real-time metrics, it is important that what is being run by JMP is the latest version and not a down-level piece of code. This matters for the sake of consistency, accuracy, and precision as much as it does that the script is executing using the latest data available. For example, before running any number of scripts, a script would fetch from the DVCS the latest code version into the workspace and use those scripts to execute within JMP in the generation of metrics. In a local version control system, this would be fairly haphazardous and could result in errors or reports that are not of top quality.

CHAPTER 5

So What About a Bad Economy?

5.1 *Overachievement—Data Virtualization*

5.2 *JMP Connection as the Universal Server*

5.3 *Well-Formed Data*

5.4 *Linked Data*

Whether a business is impacted by bad economic conditions or is simply facing tough competition, there is no excuse today for not leveraging the statistical software technology to squeeze out the waste, become more operationally lean, and at the same time make the right business decisions most of the time. Not doing so is to not count additional profitability because that which goes to waste or is incidentally and summarily overlooked is a loss. It is a loss in terms of achieving lower costs, improvements to the supply chain and subsequent revenues, and added value to product for the customer, which in the end affects the valuation of the company by owners and shareholders.

JMP CONNECTIONS is a more advanced way of thinking about business metrics. Most of the solutions today for the dashboards or scorecards are web server–based models and yes they tap into a multitude of data silos, and yes the web pages look like pretty slick applications, but the work is primarily done on the server. That work does not include advanced statistical analysis unless the time and money is spent to write the programming into the back end. As a result, most of the reporting is data filtering and presentation organizational building tasks, which is quite easy to do. Even the time it takes to do that is considerable. So in reality, a better looking report may be attained but that does not necessarily get your firm to a metric level of capability that JMP is able to give an organization. In a bad economy where groups are struggling to be the best at what they do, the trade-offs must be fully understood when it comes to deciding whether a JMP CONNECTIONS platform is the direction to take versus the other solutions people are trying to build.

The in-memory statistical capability on the client side is a significant advantage. The JMP CONNECTIONS provides a balance between what takes place at the server end and puts the power in the hands of the user at the client workstation end. If the data resources available to JMP come from a single micro-data warehouse or from many other connectivity options, a certain degree of information interoperability problems resolve due to the fact that the business logic in the form of SQL, Views, Procedures, and Functions that take place server side can actually be called upon from a JMP JSL script. The balance, interoperability, and executable business logic empowers the platform for getting exactly the data set to JMP either for presentation immediately or for automatically executing a statistical formula for the end user followed by a graphical presentation. The visuals that JMP produces are also superior in terms of scale, resolution, and customization.

The added value of putting JMP CONNECTIONS as your centerpiece for BI competency is the fact that it is also going to make the people in your organization smarter. Any tool that is able to communicate a better understanding of the problem or allows the end user to experiment with his or her ideas after generating the metric is a win-win! The web-based paradigm assumes that the developers writing to a fixed specification know what the end users want; after all, they gathered user requirements, right? Even though there may be a number of viewing options, there is no flexibility to allow the end user to massage the information. JMP has exactly the appeal with regard to a spreadsheet that has what-if analysis or goal seeking built in or at least available to the end user as an analytic option. JMP is exponential in that regard because of all the easy-to-use statistical functions. It is also easy because the JMP table is an analogue to the spreadsheet and therefore easily understood by a majority of people in business.

The natural tendency and human nature is for people to shy away from or avoid metrics. Doing so today means you probably should not be in business. Bold embrace of metrics should go all the way from the production floor right up to the top, the owner or executive. Great metrics allows a business man or woman to use their best judgment, experience, and even their gut feel when several alternatives are available or when imperfect data is present at the time for making decisions. Once the JMP CONNECTIONS starts to integrate into the business environment, the tendency for people to avoid metrics decreases because it becomes less of an intellectual barrier whereby they realize it makes their jobs easier. A great easy-to-understand metric is the whole point; the easier a job becomes, the higher the productivity.

Unlike a web server–based metric generation system, JMP facilitates exposure of the codified business logic, whereas on the web server–based model, the logic and code is all hidden and abstracted from the enterprise as a whole. It remains under the control of the IT department, and the reason[1] a back-end server-based system is not a good thing is it does not allow for easy reuse or access by statisticians, engineers, or the consumers of the KPIs if ad hoc analysis is desired. In developing a knowledge asset that takes the form of a JMP JSL script, multiple SQL statements can be integrated into the script code, tailored or customized logic can operate on the data, and presentation of the metrics is more or less a trivial exercise at that point. Needless to say, the asset is available for reuse.

The sole purpose for creating a bevy of knowledge assets is to be able to reuse, share, and manage them. The end-user community can inspect, validate, and begin to build a linked data infrastructure across the enterprise. Why is this important in a lousy economy? It is important because time is of the essence when it comes to answering questions about the state of affairs in an ongoing concern. The answers required are needed now, or as soon as it is practical to obtain. But in most cases, no one has an answer or the answers come too late. Being able to get an answer on-demand is perhaps the ultimate achievement of this intellectual journey.

Performance degradation issues add up across an enterprise and must be overcome especially when economic conditions are testing companies to their limits. The nice thing about developing through the levels of capability is the more you see, the more you want of it. The next section discusses the more advanced working possibilities of the platform.

5.1 OVERACHIEVEMENT—DATA VIRTUALIZATION

SUPERIOR DATA—OR SIMPLY DATA VIRTUALIZATION

As the JMP CONNECTIONS Level 2 capability matures, something very subtle begins to take place that is essential for getting to the Level 3

---

[1] "Reason is the non-contradictory integration of experience."—Nathaniel Branden

capability with the production of metrics. The micro-data warehouse as it resides on the data virtualization server MySQL database depicted in Figure 5.1 on page 112 as a unified data store actually becomes the development platform for the BI analyst. The warehouse is inclusive in the use of the tools such as the phpMyAdmin database administration application, JMP Pro, and Emacs editor utilized for writing code and testing the scripts and functions to generate the metric.

The real overachievement is the fact that a data virtualization server (DVS) is being constructed as more and more metric entities are developed and deployed. The structuring and build of the DVS is simply a consequence of creating views, software as a service to the platform in the form of database functions and procedures. What happens is the micro-data warehouse concept becomes less of a database or data warehouse and more of a powerful composite from which JMP Pro does its mining. (See Figure 5.1.)

Data virtualization is the presentation of data as an abstract layer, independent of underlying database systems, structures, data silos, and storage. In this case, regardless of the number of virtual connectivity options available to JMP Pro from the universe of data silos in Figure 3.12, JMP Pro can now operate against the DVS as though it is a single connection. The DVS is configured to make the connections to the various data resources.

The centerpiece of the hub connectivity is JMP Pro. With this architecture, more and more work can be loaded upon this platform where optimizing via task scheduling of scripts is the primary driver for reducing FTEs. The output side of the hub with regard to visualization or presentation in portal formats is left up to enterprise consumer's preferences.

The mistake often made is that when there are many data silos, applications, and databases to draw from, people want to create another data warehouse. In many cases, data feeding into JMP CONNECTIONS may be coming from a data warehouse already. So does it really make sense to data warehouse into another data warehouse?

As the virtualized abstraction layer develops, the problem of data integration resolves as a result of defining the metric and testing the logic to execute its generation. Simply, key factors for data virtualization include agility, flexibility, prototyping, real-time data, and fast

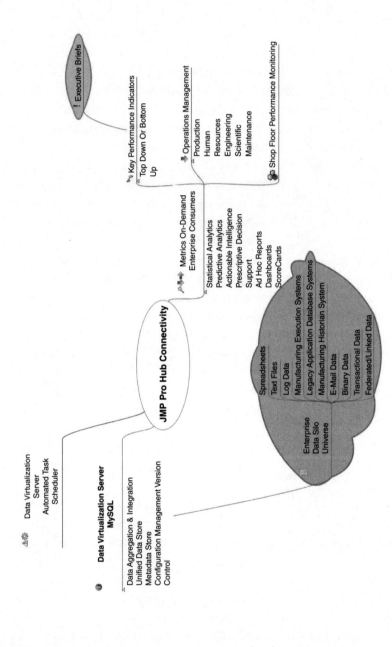

Figure 5.1 Data Virtualization Server

response. Taking a data warehouse approach implies a CAPEX size project with all the SDLC work that comprises. The initial premise though for the JMP CONNECTIONS platform was to illustrate how an intellectual work production of metrics can be developed and deployed for minimal expenses. So the incremental rollout of metrics starting with those prioritized as most critical or those making a rapid return on the investment will over a short time provide for a very powerful business asset embodied in the DVS.

A key feature for having a DVS is the fact that it has a high degree of self-maintenance. If a true data warehouse is built from disparate data sources, the data warehouse has the inherent problem of keeping the warehouse current, which includes problems with IT infrastructure performance and bandwidth issues to either constantly or periodically refresh the warehouse, particularly from those external transaction-based application database systems.

The DVS is optimized with regard to connectivity to the data repositories. Once a view is created and resides on the DVS, it automatically maintains its data currency. The view enables data currency as an important capability as far as JMP Pro script execution is concerned in support of on-demand metrics delivery. Another example of this would be a Microsoft SQL server as a linked server configuration that essentially provides the micro-data warehouse a VIEW, also known as a federated table, to an external MS SQL server database silo. The view and the federated table is a leap forward, alleviating what previously may have been a manual task.

The BI analyst must make a determination with regard to what makes sense regarding the components that need to go into the DVS. Real-time streaming data would not be a candidate; as an example, the OSISoft Product PI Historian data better resides on its own servers and a direct connection from JMP Pro would be more practical depending on the metric and the semantics it is to represent.

Virtualizing data on a Level 3 capability would further enable utilization of JMP Pro advance predictive analytic features. Typically, statistical analysis in predictive work requires a larger volume of data as well as a wider bandwidth of data attributes. For example, to apply predictive analytics to equipment reliability monitoring in a TPM program beyond just OEE, the BI analyst would incorporate with OEE, data from the MES, PI Historian data, and original equipment manufacturer's (OEM) parts data with respect to mean time between failures (MTBF), to name a few. Reliability is defined as the probability that a device will perform its required function under stated conditions for a specific period of time. On a complex piece of equipment, there are hundreds of variables that can affect its performance. JMP Pro would have available some subset of metric components from the DVS with perhaps a long run-time base of historical data from the machine. Using this advanced tool would help the maintenance shop estimate when to expect to perform the next preventative maintenance work to avoid unplanned downtime.

5.2 JMP CONNECTION AS THE UNIVERSAL SERVER

THE UNIVERSAL SERVER FOR VIRTUALIZING DATA

Data virtualization is not a replacement solution for creating new data warehouse projects. In fact, many times something that may be called a data warehouse is in fact just another database application simply based on the fact that it may only be handling megabytes, not terabyte volumes of data. In any case, it is far easier to think of the DVS as an extension or parallel system that enhances enterprise data management for building metrics.

To this point in the discussion, nothing has been said about the infrastructure that makes our data silos look as one when talking about the DVS as an abstraction for JMP CONNECTIONS. The JMP CONNECTION DVS becomes a universal server in the enterprise when fully deployed with limited or no manual intervention other than normal computing administration work. Figure 5.2 illustrates a low-cost solution that only requires implementation and testing to fully enable the universal server (Figure 3.4 on page 84) concept.

Having identified a metric, in this case a knowledge asset applet to monitor a water pump in a municipal treatment plant, the end result is the inclusion of a KPI in a Manufacturing Performance Intelligence report. The general presentation could come from a prefab web-based format directly from the historian database system or ideally a custom

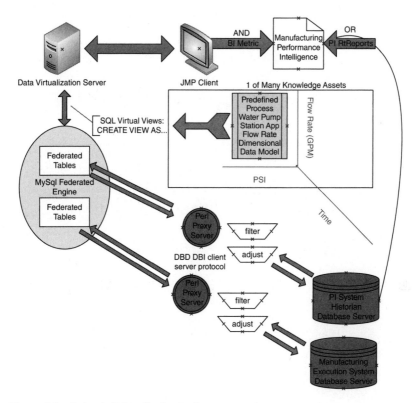

Figure 5.2 Federated Virtualization Engine

BI metric from the JMP CONNECTION client, which is most likely more meaningful. This, however, is a presentational decision with respect to the KPI deliverable.

The specification of the required metric depends on a virtual view available on the data virtualization server, for instance, a data sub-set that has been assembled for many possible uses such as statistical process control and monitoring of equipment via a JMP script. The assemblage of data depends once again on aggregation and integration. Fortunately, access to remote data is made extremely easy because the MySQL database server has what is called a *federated storage engine*. It is a storage engine that accesses data in tables of remote databases rather than in local tables. It is made to look as though other database brands are one with the MySQL database. (See Figure 5.3.)

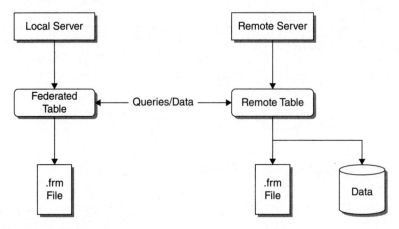

Figure 5.3 Federated Concept [15]

This federated storage engine enables data to be accessed from a remote MySQL database on a local server without using replication or cluster technology. When using a federated table, queries on the local server are automatically executed on the remote (federated) tables. No data is stored on the local tables.

There are several ways to configure federated table setups. In one such example to make this happen all you need is Perl and a couple of commonly available modules. Specifically, as a starting point you need the Perl module DBIx::MyServer, which is the link between the federated engine and a remote database. The link serves as a proxy server or man-in-the-middle because it is the client/server protocol that enables two-way communication to and from the federated engine to just about any other type of database, such as PostgreSQL/Oracle/SQL Server/SQLite/MS SQL and so forth. The Perl configuration can also interface to read file-system directories, list e-mail headers, get content from the Web, and do anything the programmer can do in Perl; one can see it through the MySQL interface. There is a rich inventory of Perl modules available for use at the CPAN code repository.

There can be as many proxy server instances as there are disparate database servers in your enterprise. The proxy server receives requests from the federated engine, passes that onto the target database, and returns the results to the federated engine. A strategic advantage of the proxy server is the opportunity to modify or manipulate a query before sending it to the target database or modify the results before sending the results back to the federated engine.

There is nothing magical about the proxy server because the protocol is actually a utilization of the appropriate ODBC driver for operative purposes to the target database server.

When the DVS executes or maintains a virtual view, it is actually operating from the federated tables as contained in the federated storage engine. This point of integration of data from multiple database servers is what enables interoperability to build the knowledge asset. There is no manual exporting and importing necessary and no data replication involved. The federated engine simply stores the definition of the table, which is identical to the table on the remote database server.

As mentioned earlier, federated tables is an easy solution to build out as there are several excellent reference resources to step an administrator through the setup process and document typical deployments. These include the following:

1. Philip Stoev > DBIx-MyServer-0.42 > DBIx:MyServer. http: //search.cpan.org/~philips/DBIx-MyServer-0.42/lib/DBIx/My Server.pm

2. The Federated Storage Engine. http://dev.mysql.com/doc/ refman/5.0/en/federated-storage-engine.html

3. MySQL as universal server by Giuseppe Maxia. http://ftp.nchu .edu.tw/MySQL/tech-resources/articles/dbixmyserver.html

4. MySQL Federated Tabels: The Missing Manual by Giuseppe Maxia. http://www.oreillynet.com/lpt/a/6679

5.3 WELL-FORMED DATA

CLEANSING, FILTERING, RESHAPING COMPUTED VALUES

Another opportunity afforded by building knowledge assets on the JMP CONNECTIONS platform is that of attaining "well-formed data." Any person who has ever tried to make a chart or graph knows quickly that data often times needs to be cleaned up and put into its proper format first. Data cleansing is expedited more readily, for example, from aggregating localized data from a spreadsheet into the micro-data warehouse, to building in constraints on the SQL statements, to also filtering within JMP. The BI analyst can never assume data to be perfect. There can be errors or missing data points and non-precise data can turn into bad information, leading to foul decision consequences.

If the JMP CONNECTIONS platform can support an inventory of knowledge assets, there must be some congruence with the decision processes taking place dynamically on a daily basis across the enterprise. If knowledge assets facilitate the linkage of information, the decision processes will be much improved. Decision processes are linked and have dependencies and are known as *decision streams*, especially when decisions are made sequentially as may happen in a batch production system.

Between the concepts of well-formed data and outright data errors, missing data, and data lacking in precision is the interrogative idea of just exactly how does one measure things? While developing a metric and even after it is in use for awhile, it is not so uncommon to come upon the realization that there may be multiple ways to compute a result. When companies have data silos and a thorough understanding of ambiguities in the meaning of the data that are discovered across the various data tables, it starts to dawn on the BI analyst there is more than one way to calculate a measurement. Ambiguous results can be especially problematic when the data is to be used in many places or product lines across a manufacturing enterprise.

For example, a paint manufacturing operation is probably a batch process type of concern. The company is having a difficult time delivering product on time to their distributors. As a result the managers want to monitor how long it takes to release each batch of paint from start to finish. The way they go about measuring the interval is to record the final batch release date obtained from the quality department and subtract the batch start date recorded by the production department. The master recipes vary but generally indicate the batch formally starts when the first two ingredients are combined. The planning department assumes the batch starts when they release the recipe to the production department. Sometimes the planning department releases more than one recipe at a time in order to keep the production lines running over weekends and holiday periods when planning personnel are off. Depending on whom you talk to at the paint company, discrepancies become obvious. These types of issues may need to be piloted when developing the metric to establish what is the best practice time that one should be measuring against. And, it will become necessary to meet with the respective parties to explain and come to an agreement when people have different assumptions.

In any case, working to refine the final metric leads to well-formed data that has a consensus between the users and where the data is sourced to produce it.

Well-formed data leading to a highly refined metric has extensibility. For example, if the office secretary ordered takeout from a restaurant and the restaurant delivered only to find out that they messed up the order or left something out of the bag, obviously the restaurant did not get it "right the first time" (RFT). In any other environment, a root cause investigation might turn up a series of deviations from normal performance of processing orders. A refined metric that tracks deviations in an effort to do a better job, decrease waste, and deliver the product or service right the first time every time can easily be extended to predict or forecast the potential number of deviations. While this may not be significant for a small operation, it is definitely an asset to an organization that may generate hundreds of nonconforming incidences through their production cycles. A forecast can give managers and planners an approximate idea of how much manpower it will take to investigate, correct, and close their deviation workload. Trending through the forecast should show over time better performance as corrective actions are put in place. Forecasting can be as simple as utilizing a uniform weighted moving average (UWMA) formula in JMP to project into the future. As RFT improves, so does customer satisfaction. In the case of a restaurant being a small business, RFT is significant for customer retention and repeat business. One mistake by not getting the order right the first time is enough to lose a customer for good. Extensibility is an important factor in maintaining smooth error-free operations in a tough economy for almost every business.

5.4 LINKED DATA

STRUCTURED DATA INTERLINKAGE HAS LINEAGE

This section, Linked Data, could well be the most important piece of information in this book. As a capstone to JMP CONNECTIONS, it is significant because the result or outcome described here can make the difference between mediocre performance and exceptional profitability achievement. From the perspective of the end user of metrics and KPIs, linked data as described in this section shows no concrete examples or ways in which this helps to make a metric better or helps the end user make a better decision. It is a black box when viewing the outputs from the JMP CONNECTIONS platform at 50,000 feet. What Section 5.4 imparts are the clear box details at the bottom of the platform's technical food chain that goes a step beyond simply having well-formed data to data that is structured for use in delivering data sets to JMP that otherwise could not be derived from other systems such as relational database systems.

As the DVS matures and the data gets refined, the BI analyst being close to and understanding the data should come to realize something different about the data. That realization is the fact that across the virtualized data environment, there is a "data lineage," or in other words data items are linked to other data items. When data resides in a relational database, the predicate (aka properties) relationships are not obvious, nor are they present because the entities or schema that are the structures within a database application lack meaning or semantics. There are a number of reasons the analyst may come to this realization. Sooner or later, one tries to pull together a data set for use in JMP and finds that perhaps a key data element is not so easy to retrieve. The last resort is always the manual copy-and-paste approach, but that defeats our purposes here to try to automate the production of metrics. Ambiguity may be another reason in that naming conventions used to identify data elements may hinder one's ability to write a concise SQL statement or business logic in the SQL statement to draw out the desired data. Another example in manufacturing is "batch genealogy" whereby information is like an ancestry genealogy—the hierarchical relationships can go pretty deep. Beyond one or two levels of hierarchy it gets more and more difficult to resolve how the data is connected or related in a relational database form.

In order to harvest hard to find and retrieve data, the data has to be structured. Once it is structured it then becomes truly "linked data." Linked data can then be queried in ways not available to us in a relational database application.

To make this capstone for the JMP CONNECTIONS platform, a transformation using semantic technologies applied using the virtualized enterprise data can be a supplemental component of the micro-data warehouse. One can think of this transformation as data reshaping before actually using it to build a target metric.

In order to house the structured data, installing a graph database server on the DVS is in order. A graph database is a database that uses graph structures with nodes, edges, and properties to represent and store data. The data model for structuring data is the Resource Description Framework (RDF). The document of reference for RDF from the W3C is located at http://www.w3.org/TR/rdf-concepts/.

Resource Description Framework was originally a framework for representing information on the World Wide Web. In the reference document "Resource Description Framework (RDF): Concepts and Abstract Syntax," Introduction and Sections 1 through 3 are explanatory in terms of why it fits at this point into this discussion. Graph theory from the study of mathematics or computer science is the study of graphs, which are mathematical structures used to model pairwise relations between objects. Many practical problems can be represented by graphs and can be used to model many types of relations and processes in physical, biological, social, and information systems.

It is easier to visualize the proposed usage in the JMP CONNECTIONS platform with an example. Take a very large cookie manufacturing enterprise. The factory equipment is capable of making and packaging many types of very tasty cookies for all seasons of the year. Cookies are made with recipes via batch processes and it is very easy to change from a Quebec Maple-Pecan to a Pumpkin Spiced Iced Cookie. The factory can take special orders or fulfill private label brands. From the start of manufacture to delivering the cookies to the customer, the data is linked. In other words one should be able to trace what ingredients went into producing the final product including the attributes such as measured amounts, weight, type, etc., for each operational step of the process such as mixing time, temperature, and baking information. This traceability is data lineage or in this case batch heritage. In order to view lineage information no matter where you are at in the process, batch analysis ideally could be navigated either upward or downward to see where ingredients or additives were used. The graph data model for structured manufacturing data is the opportunity for traversal, query, and returning result sets back for consumption to perform JMP statistical analysis. Hypothetically, if the cookie factory's dough-making department turns out 12 different types of dough as raw material used in all the various recipes, one should be able to generate a graphical view, a hierarchical lineage table, or queried result set of where a specific batch of dough was used in all the various types of cookies that were produced. If a batch of cookies turned out to be a batch of crumbs, maybe the wrong dough was used for that particular recipe. While this example is simplistic, the graph data model works for even the most complex lineage scenarios.

To quickly gain confidence in undertaking the idea of this suggested capstone, the following steps can be taken to implement structuring your data:

1. Install a graph database on the DVS server.
2. Select a data set for modeling.
3. Edit a file to structure the data from the model as RDF triples to a file.
4. Determine if the model makes sense in terms of subject, predicate, and object or literal relationships and entailment or linkage.
5. Create a script to read from the virtualized data environment.
6. The script should iterate through the data to structure it as modeled.
7. The script should write the structured triples to the graph database.
8. Query the graph database to return a result set in a table for use by JMP.

In Step 3 above, the edited RDF file can be opened by a semantic web browser to view the model graphically. This intermediate step is a review to figure out if the semantics being used in the model makes sense in the real world. Starting with Step 5, what the script logic does is "RDF-izing" or mapping the micro-data warehouse data into the structure that represents the real-world object or domain knowledge. What is not immediately obvious about RDF triples but quickly becomes evident is that triples link to other triples by way of the RDF formalism or syntax often stated as XML serialization syntax by semantic practitioners. There are tools available that may work in place of a customized script such as D2RQ, Virtuoso, Triplify, R20, and Dartgrid for mapping relational data to RDF. But the purpose of examining a small data model initially is to aid in understanding how the model can leverage data that is unstructured and disconnected in the micro-data warehouse by reshaping it through a graph database to produce useful results table for JMP from the graph. Literally, from the end-to-end data lineage in the cookie factory, this is really thinking in terms of a totally integrated supply chain ontology.

To make this even more simple, let's say you are in the cookie development lab or your own kitchen at home and you invented a new cookie recipe. If we think the cookies are going to be a big hit with our customers, we can partake in Steps 2 and 3 by modeling our data. With any given recipe there is more than one way to model the data and it may depend on the expressiveness of the recipe itself, and a certain amount of learning goes into the workup of the model. The two graphs in Figures 5.4 and 5.5 depict what the data looks like after it is structured and drawn on a canvas in the semantic Web browser.

The batch number is CM6070 and it was prepared on November 23, 2013. The ingredient list is clearly displayed and an example of linked data indicates that CM6070 used dry, wet, and add-in materials from the available stock of ingredients. CM6070 also links to another node on the graph via a green line to the measurement data for each ingredient for this recipe. There is also a subtle modeling error in Figure 5.4; see if you can pick it out.

This area of the graph looks very busy even though the ingredients come from a very small recipe. Not only does this network show the unit of measure and the value for each ingredient, it also shows the type, which we would presume to come from the raw materials inventory or stock. Every data model can be further refined; however, that usually means a consensus by subject matter experts as to the meaning and relationships this model represents. So for example, if

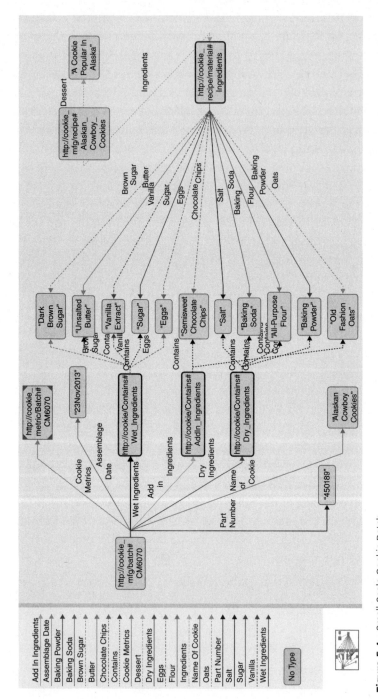

Figure 5.4 Small-Scale Cookie Batch

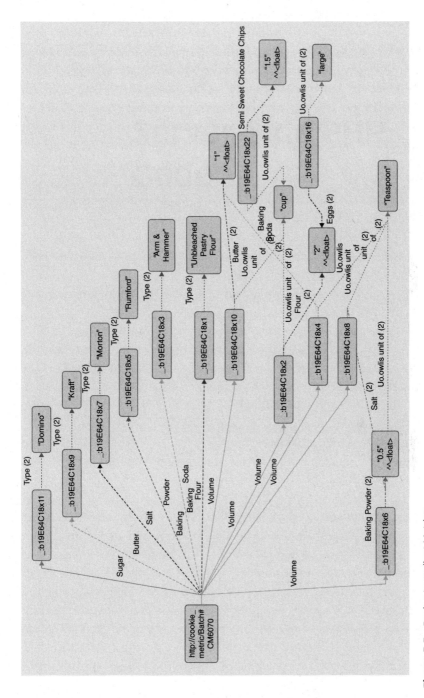

Figure 5.5 Recipe Ingredient Metrics

125

the recipe calls for two eggs, the predicate for its unit of measure is probably not the word volume; rather the word size should be used because people know eggs to be small, medium, large, or extra large. The structured data utilized to generate these graphs can be found in Appendix D. It consists of 86 triples containing 61 nodes and 86 links.

Additional RDF models could be generated and saved to RDF files for such things as preparation processing by operations such as combining, mixing, and baking. If you had a need to drill down even further, you could model the data associated with a particular raw material and its specifications. In order to visually traverse the network of data within the browser, clicking on the next node to display its subject or object illustrates the ease of tracing the materials and its properties.

Once the data has been structured, additional ways to view the data are available. The two graphics in Figures 5.6 and 5.7 show a navigable hierarchical and a tabular format.

The Value column data in Figure 5.7 is clickable for expansion of property descriptions as well.

Once the model is complete, a short script can be written to read all the batch record data from the micro-data warehouse to form the triples, and the triples would be saved to the Graph Database as mentioned in Step 7. Running this script as a scheduled task periodically would refresh the Graph Database as new data is virtualized in the warehouse.

Finally, Graph Database queries can be executed to generate exactly the data table set that was so impossible to get from the micro-data warehouse even though its data has been aggregated and integrated. Unfortunately, JMP does not have a feature to be able to directly query the Graph Database like it does with a standard relational database through the use of an ODBC driver. An ODBC driver is a programming language middleware API. The driver can be viewed as a translation layer for communicating with a database management system. It passes database queries between an application and the database. Consequently because of the lack of a programming interface between JMP and a Graph Database, the query has to take place on the Graph Database. The result set can be returned as another graph (i.e., triples) or a csv file for further processing by JMP or saved

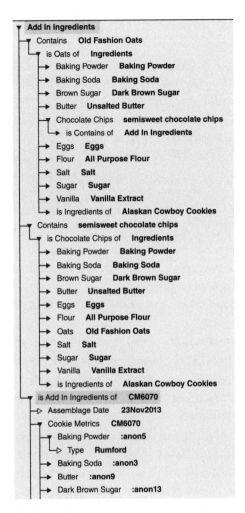

Figure 5.6 Hierarchical Data Format

to the micro-data warehouse where JMP could then access it via script execution.

A side comment, linked data connection methods are somewhat similar to ODBC in that a URI is somewhat similar to a connection string required by ODBC connection initiation, and the Semantic Web Query Language (SPARQL) being somewhat similar to SQL through the established connection.

CM6070	
Property	Value
Add In Ingredients	Add In Ingredients
Assemblage Date	23Nov2013
Cookie Metrics	CM6070
Dry Ingredients	Dry Ingredients
Name Of Cookie	Alaskan Cowboy Cookies
Part Number	450189
Wet Ingredients	Wet Ingredients

Figure 5.7   Cookie Data in a Table Format

Extending the theory that linked data is somewhat analogous to ODBC, it would be possible to establish an ODBC connection to a linked data store (such as a "triple store") and send SPARQL queries down an ODBC connection. OpenLink Virtuoso allows you to connect via the standard ODBC connection; however, there has not been any testing thus far using the Virtuoso driver with JMP and sending SPARQL queries to any of the popular graph databases through the Virtuoso driver. Alternatively, one other last method of data access using SPARQL queries that could take place without a driver would be SPARQL Over HTTP (SOH). In JMP scripting, using the Open(..) API, access to a web server hosting a data store that supports SOH may contain the query appended to the URL. The protocol and standards for this type of communication with a data store are documented in http://www.w3.org/TR/sparql11-query/, the W3C title "SPARQL 1.1 Query Language." Graph Database server products that support SOH include Apache Jena, the "Fuseki: Serving RDF data over HTTP" project at http://jena.apache.org/documentation/serving_data/, and AllegroGraph 6.2.1 HTTP Protocol product by The Franz Company at http://www.franz.com/agraph/support/documentation/current/http-protocol.html.

As is so often the case in making a product, it is necessary to monitor the process, conduct statistical process control, and later perform modeling and simulation capabilities. In going from the current state to a new capability maturity model in support of our business, the new competency gains include a target for real-time production of metrics and predictive analytics for NOW-casting, forecasting, and achieving RFT objectives, given the identification and refinement of key metrics. To improve the graph data model it may be appropriate to pull from the micro-data warehouse test data taken from samples during the preparation process operations and structure it, which might include testing on purity of ingredients, sterile water, taste, appearance, temperature, and texture to name a few. For statistical process control, critical or key quality attributes are important. Coming from the Graph Database may enable more advance analytic capabilities.

In review, a focus on data input storage and data reshaping, or more to the point, graph databases and graph operations, respectively provisions an intermediate step of taking aggregated data and reshaping it as connected data. This transformation accomplishes a number of objectives that are a means to an end. The end game is to quickly and repeatedly achieve a data set for use by JMP.

The transformation takes from various sources data input and structures the data for storage into the graph database. A graph database stores data in a graph, the most generic of data structures, capable of elegantly representing any kind of data in a highly accessible way. The objectives of the transformation include the following:

1. Formalized reshaping via data modeling to give meaning (i.e., semantic composition) to the raw aggregate or metadata.

2. Structuring means the data is no longer aggregated; rather it has a connectedness referred to as linked data where properties and relationships are defined.

3. Enables the ability to query a graph. A traversal is how you query a graph, navigating from starting nodes to related nodes according to an algorithm, finding answers to questions, returning data set results.

4. Transformed into a knowledge asset in support of a KPI metric.

What makes it a knowledge asset? The answer to this question is once the data takes the form of a graph, there are many standard recognizable traversal patterns in these networks. If you combine together RDF files or put triples into the Graph Database and the graph is connected, the graph as a whole is a single atomic data structure. The analog to the traversal would be business logic executed on a relational database application encapsulated in a structured query language statement run against the database. The classical difference between these two different methods can dawn on one via the following paraphrase:

> A relational database may tell you the average age of everyone in this place, but a graph database will tell you who is most likely to buy you a beer. (Andreas Kollegger, Neo4J)

With the RDF data model where the semantics of properties and relationships are integrated, it can show the following:

1. Where the data comes from
2. Where it flows
3. How it is transformed as it travels through the enterprise

It has been said (another management adage),

> You can't manage what you can't find.

Thus the data models as graph representations are a way to document where the data is, how it flows so you can manage it and secure it appropriately as it moves across the corporate network. So whether a firm is audited internally or externally for utilization of its data, structured data technology puts us in a stronger position to justify compliance particularly when it is necessary for regulatory requirements.

As mentioned previously, to query the graph database is to traverse it for a result. SPARQL (pronounced "sparkle," a recursive acronym for SPARQL Protocol and RDF Query Language) is an RDF query language, that is, a query language for databases, able to retrieve and manipulate data stored in Resource Description Framework format and readily available for use to retrieve the appropriate data set to satisfy the requirements to do calculation as an RDF object; data can be of a numeric type and not just string literals. This will be familiar to programmers that write relational database SQL.

The benefits associated with having this capstone include the following:

1. Increase utilization of data for running a more efficient business.
2. Improve the quality and accuracy of the data prior to analytics and reporting.
3. Reduce the risk associated with manual data input.
4. Provision real-time metric from a more complex knowledge asset.
5. Discoverability and reasoning.

At the beginning of Section 5.4 the discussion touched upon the obvious lack of examples about how linked data concretely helps the consumer of KPI metrics. It helps in the most indirect or transparent way because JMP is a consumer of data, whereas the user of a KPI metric is a consumer of information. JMP is the transformer by taking from structured data and performing statistical processes, and the output is delivered to KPI consumers. It therefore follows that the BI analyst may be able to have a deeper appreciation for the technical aspects of linked data than would the end user of the metrics the platform produces. There are no better examples that illustrate this seeming dichotomy than web sites such as data.gov.uk (http://data.gov.uk/), the NOW website (http://now.winnipeg.ca/), and the Peg website (http://www.mypeg.ca) whereby an open semantic framework with linked data as its foundation is never apparent to the Peg user community, yet is integral in serving some 54 data sets representing more than 4,000 different entities. [10]

For additional technical and explanatory reading, Leigh Dodds' blog article titled "The Benefits of Linking Data" at http://data.gov.uk/blog/the-benefits-of-linking-data is one of the clearest explanations of the meaning and benefits of linking data.

CHAPTER 6

Decision Streams

ONLY AS GOOD AS YOUR LAST DECISION

Another facet about decisions and the impact the process has on results is the fact that no single decision in a typical day when made correctly or optimally necessarily will reflect on performance. Many good decisions, whether small, medium, or large over a quarter, season, or campaign, should and will have a positive exponential effect on the management of corporate performance. Think of decisions in terms of good and bad streams on the order of a laminar flow water jet [39]. When all the molecules are going in the same direction parallel to each other, it is a beautiful thing. A series of bad decisions is the opposite, having negative consequences for corporate performance management (CPM).

Are firms doing accounting on the countless decisions that are made each day? Are firms tracking decisions in an aggregated statistical manner over time within the context of categorical attributes such as criticality, impact/risk, relationships, geo proximity, valuation, outcomes, and so forth? Perhaps only military organizations conduct these types of analysis in their training and real-time evaluations of the battle space.

Much depends on the type of decision, whether you are talking about programmed or non-programmed decision-making activities. There are many good slide presentations on the Web for a general overview. No matter what the decision environment or scope, better information and knowledge brings about better decisions. In most any business today the Occupational Safety and Health Administration (OSHA) has special emphasis on a domain within CPM. In practical terms, a firm that has no policies and procedures in place and decides to implement a corporate-wide program is probably a good decision. It is a good decision because by statistically demonstrating and achieving high standards on an annual basis, liability insurance premiums will stay low, a KPI in CPM. So, the decision to go forward with initiatives causes a cascade of decisions in the firm from top to bottom. Decision accounting comes in the form of monitoring. Before giving an example about monitoring, an exemplary company that takes health, safety, and environment (HSE) seriously is Halliburton (http://www.halliburton.com/en-US/about-us/hse-sq.page?node-id=hgeyxt64)

and visiting their site will leave no doubt in anyone's mind that they are monitoring their HSE data to evaluate performance and conformance to company policy. They clearly state that solving customer challenges is second only to the HSE program.

For example, it might be decided that security and safety audits would be conducted in all areas. As a result of this decision, employees document or count all security issues and safety hazards. At Halliburton the goal is "ZERO."

> The goal of ZERO is to take significant steps in improving our HSE and service quality performance. ZERO was implemented in 2011 and drives to reduce safety incidents, environmental incidents and nonproductive time, with a goal of ZERO [12].

The information gathered would cause management to refine their decisions and modify the policy to require that a certain percentage of all the problems uncovered will be remediated within certain number of days. What good does it do find a problem if it is not fixed? Thus, the statistics trickle back up the chain of command whereby the CPM group sets an ambitious goal for site safety of less than or equal to some percentage goal (i.e., "ZERO" for Halliburton) of total recordable incidents computed using the U.S. Department of Labor's formula (http://www.bls.gov/iif/osheval.htm) for the year. It is no stretch of anyone's imagination to know that if you make your workplace a safer place, you would expect to have fewer employees injured on the job, assuring a certain constant level of human productivity. Halliburton takes this a step further by associating the HSE performance to what they call service quality performance. A zero incidence safety record translates to a quality of service they are able to provide to their customers, perhaps the highest in their industry.

These decision streams seem very concrete and straightforward. In Halliburton's case, they decided upon ZERO, 10 Life Rules and Safety Moments to promote HSE throughout the enterprise.

In the HSE scenario, decision process improvement may be the mechanism that drives a firm toward zero recordable safety incidents. In order to do this, though, the firm must embark upon building knowledge assets. In this case, data recorded will be better stored as well-formed data. The asset grows over time from month to month as records are maintained for trending and review. The knowledge asset will be linked to other safety and security knowledge assets such as near misses.

What are the crossroads of decision making? Most often these may be decisions made by individuals, technicians, or managers as they go about their daily work. On the other hand, where the cognitive work actually appears most evident is during meetings between individuals or groups within the enterprise and is often where metrics play a key role on decision streams. Collectively, decision streams are the factors driving whether an enterprise reaches their strategic goals to achieve competitive advantage over others in their industry. The decision-making process from a cognitive perspective must be regarded as a continuous process integrated in the interaction with the environment, which seems synonymous with continued process improvement. The analysis of individual decisions is concerned with the logic of decision making and rationality, a normative perspective. Being a mental process, it results in the selection of a course of action among several alternative scenarios. Every decision-making process produces a final choice, which can be an action or an opinion of choice.

With the coming together of minds in a meeting, the metrics aid in the problem analysis that may be prerequisite to a decision point. One decision can of course cascade as intended or unintended consequences into other sets of decisions or decision streams. Said another way, taking a course of action may and usually does result in another set of decisions required to arrive at a result.

Implementing a BI Competency Center works to harmonize the knowledge assets in congruence with the decision streams. In situations where mergers or buyouts occur, there is much flux taking place, and it may take years for an IT department to integrate systems. Even if a firm does not undergo a merger, how many times on an annual basis do people face the same problems over and over again? The classic example is "What should we produce and how much of it do we make?" Going back to Chapters 4 and 5, Harvesting Benefits and a Bad Economy, the JMP CONNECTIONS will be able to bring solid resolutions to reoccurring problems. Those will be hurdles removed that hold back optimal performance. The reason here is, as BI analysts work through the development of the platform and begin to build the knowledge assets, it opens their eyes in terms of identifying where the problems are coming from. So rather than guessing about whether some process should be improved with a process improvement project, they will have solid information to make recommendations and the ability to monitor the success of a green belt project before, during, and upon completion.

As per JMP their statistical discovery software contains automated analytic techniques for data mining and predictive modeling. You get the power of data visualization, exploratory data analysis, and data mining in an in-memory, desktop-based environment that provides some of the following capability:

1. Use cross-validation, bootstrap forests, boosted trees, neural networks, and stepwise regression to build more reliable predictive models.
2. Get exact measures of association for categorical analysis.
3. Run nonparametric exact tests for one-way analysis of variance.
4. Perform rapid visual comparison of competing model types.
5. Uncover variable influence for black-box techniques like random forests.

As the JMP CONNECTIONS platform matures, BI analysts and statisticians should work toward constructing predictive models. Not only is predictive modeling a pathway toward making better decisions, it will also enhance decision streams. There still is the caveat with regard to the phenomenon of people wanting to avoid metrics, especially as the complexity increases. It is advisable that as the platform goes through its maturity process, the target audience should come along with it in terms of training so that people understand the purpose, meaning, and method of use or interpretation. Just as an OEE control chart may be meaningless to an operator in production, it is very informative to engineering or maintenance. The target audience needs to be identified and calibrated to the work of the BI team, otherwise no value is added for the enterprise if no one is using their work product. The target or end-user audience is most critical when entering into advance predictive analytic projects.

CHAPTER **7**

Delivery and Presentations

Probably the most satisfying aspect of this entire solution is the ability to give people the actionable intelligence as knowledge formed from the metrics. Delivery options are many and varied. Initially, the platform seems like a good candidate for a virtual command-and-control center where you find all the action. However, the control center may serve only a few people unless there is a notification system that notifies the right people just in time when it really matters on a critical KPI. But given the idea of virtualized delivery, the platform may also serve senior management located in remote areas around the globe such that they may access the console for on-demand metrics. Remote access is known as *virtual network computing* (VNC).

7.1 PUSH VERSUS PULL DELIVERY

DELIVERY ON THE GOODS

A means of delivery or notion of *push* or *pull* could be considered a performance monitoring architecture. In simple terms, a *push* metric means metrics periodically sent by each monitored system to a central collection point such as a web portal or KPI consumer, perhaps an e-mail account. A *pull* metric is a request from central KPI collection point or consumer periodically requesting metrics from each monitored system.

Rather than the BI analyst team directing how metrics are to be delivered to their user base, the analysis should find out the preference from each of their customers. In addition, much depends on the metric itself. A reason careful consideration of delivery methods should be decided upon is that finding information faster and delivering it prevents the decision process from stalling.

In one example where a firm suffered an emergency crisis, following the crisis an enterprise corporate security consulting firm developed for their client a web application designed for Early Warning, Business Continuity, and Crisis Management command centers. Originally prototyped for a multinational corporation in the automobile manufacturing business, the Early Warning web applet was a specific BI application for corporate internal security and safety operations. Essentially operators and security analysts located in the command center gathered data from both external open sources and internal sources pertaining to the company, and it was a classified management task. The management task was considered classified in the sense that the application could do the following extremely well:

1. Rank and prioritize warnings.
2. Automatically update the criticality (rank) of warnings.
3. Selectively push warnings based on ranking and matching criteria.
4. Create highly customized push and pull conditions for delivering to the right people at the right time.
5. Quickly elaborate with more detailed information as well as its source.

The chief security officer for the firm was responsible for delivering a daily brief to the CEO by 8:00 AM every day. The action by the officer would be an example of a pushed delivery method due to the critical nature of the decision makers' growing need for reducing the information overload and for obtaining targeted, actionable, early warning intelligence. A sample summary brief is included in Appendix F.

By means of proprietary algorithms, the application reduced dramatically the noise-to-signal ratio of time-sensitive intelligence and prioritized early warnings based on relevance and criticality. Eventually, customized content and delivery went out to approximately 200 executives at all manufacturing locations, encompassing not only new threats but also social media monitoring and corporate reputation management intelligence.

The push method of delivery, no matter whether it is a text message, e-mail, hard copy brief, or web page, implies a certain urgency. For example, if parts for a manufacturing plant in Houston delivered by rail become potentially interrupted by a rail transportation strike, the head of operations would typically get advanced warning and a probability with respect to the likelihood of occurrence. The business contingency plans could be implemented to prevent a plant shutdown due to a lack of raw materials for just-in-time delivery of parts.

Utilizing a push delivery for a metric requires an acute sense of what could be too much information coming at the person. Too much information desensitizes people, and what may one day be an important metric gets ignored. Defining that fine line between what should be pushed versus a metric that is or should be monitored must be understood within the context of its usefulness. A pushed metric is more like an alarm situation. So for example, if a piece of security data was being tracked and its criticality ranking elevated, no person is required to keep an eye on it in real time. However, someone is designated for notification by the system when a parameter exceeds a certain range above its set point. In the case of early warning intelligence, the CEO is left to make judgement calls or take decisions based on ranking, relevance, criticality, probability, and time. Data that is generated and charted in real time is more likely utilized by operators for controlling a process and is thus used in real time. An example would be air traffic controller monitoring flight data and radar for handling commercial airline traffic. The data is neither a push nor a pull of information since it is constantly monitored.

The pull method of delivering metrics is the most useful for the majority of people because it is all about the notion of making metrics available on-demand. On-demand means that at any given time, the metric must already have been generated against the most current data available to date. If it is not the case, then the metric should automatically and instantly generate with very little lag time upon the demand for it.

Methods of pull when instantiated by a user might simply have the system e-mail the metric. As metrics are generated, they can be placed in a single location on a file server, hosted on an internal or intranet website, or put into a document management system for everyone to access. Once again, delivery preferences are why it is important to find out what your base of users prefer for delivery. Getting users' preferences may actually be more work than setting up the JMP CONNECTIONS platform to service delivery.

Figure 7.1 Senders push and receivers pull

In summary, implementing a push methodology is more expensive in terms of administrative overhead and maintenance. Over time as recipients change jobs or roles, address books must be kept up to date as well as making sure to control access of sensitive information to those on the receiving end of the push. The push delivery tends to be more deployable as an automated process for generating the metrics than the pull delivery mode. Keep in mind that teams of people on a production floor, in a conference room, or in a board room more likely favor the latest and greatest metrics pushed. On the other hand, when data availability is asynchronous, people prefer to pull the metric on-demand when data does become available for analysis. The delivery mechanism can be fined-tuned for your customer through the use of triggers to generate on an event as opposed to a metric generated by a task scheduler. (See Figure 7.1.)

7.2 PRESENTATION

SHOWTIME

Presentation, while it seems trivial compared to the effort that it takes to build the knowledge assets, is an important ingredient for the success and acceptance of a data virtualization platform. Visualization is the centerpiece of the JMP software. Visuals wake up the brain to conceive new ideas, patterns, trends, and overall status. The following concepts of presentations will be discuss within this section.

- Web-Based Dashboards
- Group-Based Presentation Formats (i.e., Slide Share®, MS Power Point®, Adobe PDF®, MS Word®, or Google Docs®)
- Business Intelligence Portals
  * The Right KPI for the Right Occasion
- Mobil Metrics
- JMP Journals ...

WEB-BASED DASHBOARDS

The web-based dashboards are better known as faceted[1] analytic applications because they aggregate, organize, and summarize data from a variety of quantitative and qualitative information sources (such as transactional records, inventories, sales data, human resource information, part and product information, and so on). The more robust these are in terms of allowing users to interact with the data sets, the more back-end server programming is required to support it. This robustness is great for generating insights from a broad range of unpredictable questions that almost always come up, but in fact these systems more often than not, are simple "analytic fact-finding" mechanisms. There is no in-memory analytic capability once you have the data on your desktop.

Hold the fort! That is not to say some of these Web dashboards cannot be useful for the JMP CONNECTIONS platform because in fact JMP allows as one of its connectivity options an ability to data mine the Web through the url hyperlink protocol. So a Web dashboard can exist as just another data silo as far as the JMP BI analyst is concerned. As a quick test, hyperlink to http://www.census.gov/developers/ the U.S. government Census data, and pull the sample data into JMP using the sample url hyperlinks provided.

Using JMP JSL scripting for presentation purposes, dashboards can be created if that is what is called for by the user community. There are no limitations in that regard. As a matter of convenience, a graph builder, control chart, or overlay graphic can be easily written out to a web server and coded at the end of every script. In this way the metric can be pulled up by any employee that requires quick access for analysis or inclusion into their own dashboard presentations.

GROUP-BASED PRESENTATION FORMATS

Another set of presentations that are always required are group presentations. Metrics can be put into Microsoft Power-Point®, Slide

---

[1] Faceted Browsers are defined at the MIT Simile Project (http://simile.mit.edu/wiki/Faceted_Browser), Longwell Browser (http://simile.mit.edu/wiki/Longwell), and Flamenco (http://flamenco.berkeley.edu/) for further reading.

Share®, Adobe PDF® format, Microsoft Word®, or Google Docs® for that matter. As opposed to a single metric, some thought must go into the design and layout so that it is simply not a data dump per se where you put the onus on the user to adjust the final presentation. In fact, the user community may recommend how they want to see their presentation especially if their set of dashboard slides are updated on a weekly basis.

BUSINESS INTELLIGENCE PORTALS

It should be noted that there are numerous commercial software companies marketing business intelligence portals. Therefore, the portal paradigm is one type of presentation option for an enterprise. Portals were first introduced as front ends for primary access to data warehouse and business intelligence applications. A web portal provides a starting point or a gateway to other resources on the Internet or an intranet. A powerful open source portal was the Jetspeed Project from the Apache Software Foundation. A widely used commercial portal available is the Microsoft Share Point®. Before considering this option, one needs to become knowledgeable about this type of technology for presentation of metrics since the investment can be a considerable expenditure from development and deployment to maintaining it through its life cycle. The commercial software vendor publishing portals are primarily interested in selling and licensing their bundled solution using your data. Unfortunately, most KPIs and metrics generated within portals are usually very elementary, which is probably due in part to the end-user customers affording limited computational implementations of their data. The views offered by portals can be a combination of portlets (i.e, mini-applets), widgets, or mashups. Those of course can be generic functions from a vendor or custom Java applications written by the licensee. Often known as servlets, they provide or implement the portlet's features and functions. Located server-side and hosted most often by a Web application server such as Tomcat by the Apache Software Foundation, Tomcat is capable of running Java Servlets or JavaServer Pages (JSPs).

In light of the potential utilization of portal technology, a simpler abstraction is to take the view that metrics created by the JMP

CONNECTIONS platform become the syndicated content for the portal. Use of a portal makes particularly good sense for higher level audiences that need to review a highly refined KPI. The tendency that people have with portals is to also provide facilities to display all that raw data in many different forms, tables, filtered, sliced and diced. Most of that excess can be wasted effort if the audiences in many cases are not trained business intelligence analysts. And neither do they have the subject matter expertise from the shop floor to understand the derivative nature of the metric. The portal user will not necessarily bring to light answers to the questions a KPI poses, which is related to performance.

THE RIGHT KPI FOR THE RIGHT OCCASION

To this point in the conversation, little has been discussed about selecting the right KPI. And selecting the right KPIs actually supersedes the importance of presentation if this prerequisite has not been worked out in advance. In this subtopic, referral back to the OEE Metric Case Study will serve to illustrate some principal angles to think about. A machine is a wholesome example to elaborate aspects in thinking about selecting the best KPI as it encompasses product life management and production monitoring systems on production efficiency. While advance control charting uses OEE data to monitor a machine and prognosticate breakdowns, the contextual environment also envelops the notion that our machine can produce many types of car door body parts. It also means that at some point, defects will be detected, and as different batches of doors are stamped out, a record will be kept with respect to every batch that is set up and produced. Defects may be tracked as a KPI or more likely a minor background six sigma metric. In the case where defects are costing too much time and money in waste material or rework, investigations may take place. Some departments may track such investigations as deviations. In fact, it is more common to find automated manufacturing systems that are highly integrated with production historian systems. Rockwell Automation has an excellent proprietary white paper on the topic titled "Data Historians for Incident and Deviation Management." [7] Whether finished doors start coming off the press at a rate more slowly than what is expected as optimal or a certain aspect is out of specification, the effect is the same. Productivity or efficiency is adversely impacted.

An event may or may not be a big deal. If an incident is opened, there will be several potential root cause categories common within industry. These include man-caused such as an operator error; equipment-related; process or methods, for example, incorrectly following a work instruction; and external or environmental factors. A simple determining reason for classifying a deviation as major instead of minor would be such things as a safety issue or because of regulatory requirements. For example, if the stamping press machine started losing a large amount of hydraulic fluid, which flowed into the drains in the floor and into the environment, the company would be obligated to report the incident to the Environmental Protection Agency and conduct an incident investigation. When the volume or frequency of major incidents or deviations is too great, it might warrant a KPI for tracking these problems until things are brought under control with corrective actions and preventative actions (CAPAs).

A refined KPI, however, is more than a single data point. For example, if you give an executive a quality metric such as the percent of open deviations under investigation that are past due—in other words, deviations not closed out from investigation, that may be the wrong KPI to be delivering. The reason it could be wrong has more to do with the total number of deviations open and how many investigators are working to identify the root cause and corrective action. If it is viewed as a risk by the quality department, and the organization cannot stay ahead of the game, more than likely you need to be monitoring a different KPI to track productivity performance such as the number of FTEs required to find the root causes and maintain closure rates that keep the firm in compliance with the quality department. The real KPI is also more than a graph. The metric should graph a line that is a realistic reduction from the number of deviations generated in the previous year week by week. Typically, an objective percentage goal target would be set for a reduction by management and a stretch goal of 5% above the objective even though achieving the objective percentage goal reduction is satisfactory. In this visual way the KPI is helping everyone to understand the status of where they are at while encouraging continual operational quality as well as productivity improvement.

The short of it, the metric needs to show the variance whether good or bad so that it can be managed, whether that means comparing how the organization is doing from one year to the next with historical data or, as an example, comparing the relative performance of two identical machines producing automobile car doors.

So, stop at this point and ask yourself what could be the most infamous types of nonconformance incidents known today?

> Recent major disasters include the 1984 Bhopal, India, incident resulting in more than 2,000 deaths; the October 1989 Phillips Petroleum Company, Pasadena, TX, incident resulting in 23 deaths and 132 injuries; the July 1990 BASF, Cincinnati, OH, incident resulting in 2 deaths, and the May 1991 IMC, Sterlington, LA, incident resulting in 8 deaths and 128 injuries [5].

The successful business strategy at General Electric in 1995 was made by Jack Welch, CEO, to improve the quality of process outputs by identifying and removing the causes of defects (errors) and minimizing variability in manufacturing and business processes [38]. The central strategy was Six Sigma.

The literature regarding the selection of KPIs is prolific. The thought process surrounding the topic is even well regarded by graduate students. Authors Sergei Kaganski, Aleksei Snatkin, Marko Paavel, and Kristo Karjust in September 2013 published in the *International Journal of Research in Social Sciences* a research paper titled "Selecting the Right KPIs for SMEs Production with the SUPPORT of PMS and PLM." The paper is a short read and to the point. They introduce the topic, define what KPIs are, discuss the strategies of measuring and finding the right KPIs, and then proceed to lay out the categorization of KPIs based on manufacturing levels for product life management (PLM) and process monitoring systems (PMS) for production efficiency [31]. They cite two other sources for what are considered winning KPIs, one of which is, according to Eckerson [19], managers should pay attention to the following characteristics:

- Sparse: The fewer the KPIs, the better.
- Drillable: Users can can go deeply into detail.
- Simple: The meaning of each KPI is clear.
- Actionable: Users know how to effect results.

- Owned: There is an owner for every KPI.
- Referenced: Users can view background and context.
- Correlated: KPIs drive desired outcomes.
- Balanced: KPIs consist of financial and non-financial metrics.
- Aligned: KPIs don't disrupt each other.
- Validated: Workers can't circumvent the KPIs.

On occasion the really nice thing about reading a sourced journal article is one can quickly locate the originating source of research from the bibliography for confirmation without relying upon an Internet search. Selecting the right KPIs, the authors also cited work by M. Roberts and V. Latorre who categorized indicators according to where they should be monitored and by whom. Their tables define the classifications dovetailing nicely with this metric case study discussion and the advanced OEE topic for selecting a winning KPI.

Eckerson's article, "How to Create and Deploy Effective Metrics," is a white paper written for consumption by the commercial data warehouse marketplace and is comprehensive in its coverage of creating and deploying effective metrics. Following these guidelines should help develop the KPI sets needed for presentation development.

Key performance indicators that really matter drive performance. Even though something is measurable, an organization may not qualify the metric as a KPI. Typically, the philosophy is to limit the number of KPIs to only those that contribute toward or support an organization's objective. Many firms may generalize the set of KPIs to safety, quality, productivity, and cost for a manufacturing firm. However, there may be other KPIs at various levels of the enterprise also limited because the target audiences within require operational intelligence to execute their plans to achieve the mission and meet the expectations of the overall or higher level goals.

A KPI that works does not just materialize. It should not be so general as to be of no use to business owners, senior management, or executives who are actively running operations or executing the business plan. There are several ways in which a KPI rises to its occasion or prominence. The BI analyst will recognize these with experience. Sometimes a basic metric simply keeps getting refined over time and becomes a favorite. The information it communicates and the visual presentation gets so good that people cannot live without it. Then, you have metrics based on an objective that often has its own set of problems. Consequently, a methodology to develop it into a KPI may follow the Six Sigma DMAIC model. That is (D) Define the problem, (M) Measure the data collection step, (A) Analyze using the data to identify gaps between current performance and goal performance, (I) Improve such that one can understand what needs to be done when performance is out of criteria, and (C) Control, and is thus the reason for ongoing monitoring throughout the life cycle of the objective. In addition, if the metric is good enough to be considered a KPI, the firm should seek and find where else it could be replicated in the enterprise since it may represent a new and useful knowledge asset.

The refined KPI is really all the syndicated content that is needed in a portal. The idea of including many different views of filtered data is typically sold as "drill-down" capability. Wading deeper into the underlying data assumes that a person is going to do further statistical analysis and has the subject matter expertise and skill to explain the KPI. The higher level audience that views the KPI may not have the luxury of time to utilize drill downs.

The real drill down is linked data in the form of another lower level or supporting KPI. Taking the operator error category as an example for a hazardous chemical release, a good supporting KPI metric might be the training status of the entire production staff, which answers the question of how up to date the organization is on their training levels. If only 25% of the staff are signed off and current on their effective training program modules, the lack of being 100% trained on current best practice documentation could be the whole or part of the answer as to why people are making mistakes that cause non-conformance incidents.[2] The drill down could be considered a vertical direction, whereas a horizontal or lateral drilling of data might work better for concerns when equipment deviations are prevalent

---

[2] On the other hand, it is often very easy for organizations to find blame with training when the really difficult task of uncovering the real root cause should be accomplished.

across a manufacturing plant. The maintenance shop KPI may be more representative of machine breakdowns, calibration issues, or staffing problems and needed skill sets.

We have spoken to OEE metrics and to incident or deviation KPIs already. A third type of metric in support of the deviation metric is the sub-type known in object-oriented programming as simply *polymorphism*. Polymorphism in a computing context shares important similarities with the concept of degeneracy[3] in biology. Simply speaking, to show a correlation between KPIs, the point is to say that the correlation is supportive, not disruptive, for getting a better understanding about a situation where more than one KPI is helpful in decision making.

To illustrate this concept, another refined KPI that might be found in the cookie dough manufacturing setting is having a production record for a batch that undergoes review for correctness. Let's say these records are critical in terms of being reviewed for errors prior to a quality department signoff for either further manufacturing work (i.e., using the dough in the next process step) to be done or product release. The relationship between these two KPIs is the logic that says the fewer errors found in the batch production record, the fewer the deviations because this indicates whether we are producing the product right the first time. Oftentimes errors in the batch record require a deviation to be opened for formal investigation, which means the cookie dough product cannot be released until the quality department is completely satisfied that no product impact has occurred as a result of the deviation. At times, no single KPI metric can stand alone, in other words, two or more KPIs must have an analytical eye tuned upon them for consideration in unison. Rather than a graphic mind map diagram for modeling the thought process, let's turn to the computer science concept of polymorphism. The purpose of polymorphism is to implement a style of programming/thinking called message-passing in the computer programming literature, in

---

[3] Within biological systems, degeneracy refers to circumstances where structurally dissimilar components/modules/pathways can perform similar functions (i.e., are effectively interchangeable) under certain conditions, but perform distinct functions in other conditions.

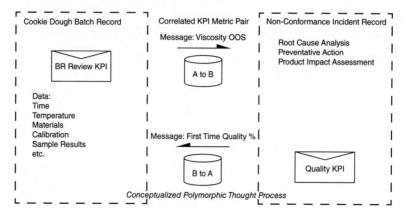

Figure 7.2 Junctured KPI Thought Process for Connecting the Dots

which objects of various types, like a quality KPI and batch record review KPI, define a so-called common interface of operations for users or in this case the consumer of these two metrics. Polymorphism usually means that type A somehow derives from type B, or type C implements an interface that represents type B. Restated, the primary deviation derives a unit of knowledge from the cookie dough batch record such that what it messages or communicates back is the *why* or reason for having a deviation. (See Figure 7.2.)

Likewise the quality KPI utilizes the unit of knowledge, the viscosity OOS indirectly, and messages its metrics back to the batch record KPI. This metric would be known as a "first time quality" (FTQ) metric. Thus, even though the batch record and the incident record are of different types and the quality KPI is a different type than the BR review KPI, both have common data connections. The thinking person can take account variables, rates of change, dependent or independent variables, or trends for monitoring or initiating improvements.

A reflective metric might look back at the previous year's record for batch record documentation errors and infer a certain level of risk associated to the number of deviation events, or, with past and current data, predict a certain number of deviations expected over the current business cycle. The lower the FTQ percentage, the more likely a rise in incidents. The polymorphism messaging concept as a thought model is key to the development of interdependent KPIs and/or associated metric drill downs, the virtual reality of CONNECTIONS as applied in this book.

In the previous discussion, one can see how and why knowledge assets can work together. For the person concerned about human resource utilization, another supporting KPI might be a deviation forecast report that aids in determining manpower requirements in managing the investigation and closure of deviations as it pertains to the less important data point of deviations past due for closure (herein referencing the classification of Roberts and Latorre for human resource KPI factor) [25], [35]. In fact, a cycle time for processing deviations is probably a more relevant data point. Given this type of presentation model, the typical drill downs to data tables are not optimal because once again, even if the portal applets have a small measure of functionality in transforming the data into a meaningful metric, it can be of little use. The applet residing in the portlet is of little functional use for browsing data, especially when one realizes that JMP is really a data browser on steroids that lends itself so well for doing the analytics. If drill downs are an absolute requirement, then if nothing else, make sure those filtered tables are directly accessible to JMP on the user's desktop without the need for exporting to spreadsheets or csv file formats.

In the final analysis, table data drill down for the deviation KPI will not lead necessarily to knowledge discovery because the production record review KPI is derived from a totally different data set even though there is linkage between the two. Portal applets in most cases are not complex enough to join tables and query based on logical business questions. If portal applets could handle more complex data presentation, that type of function would have to take place on the back-end of the portal on the server. JMP excels at making queries, creating data subsets, sorting, tabulating, computing the analytics, and ultimately generating the visual display. The knowledge asset that turns out a refined KPI is derived from structured data, not to be confused with data modeling. As it turns out, the relations between KPIs may not always be hierarchical. Rather, it appears to be more like a network of reference concepts or nodes. Knowledge assets properly constructed are also themselves part of a coherent structure where further benefits may be gained.

These benefits include inferencing, consistency testing, discovery, and navigation. For example, the deviation KPI and the production record review for the batch KPI may both be answering to a product release KPI metric whereby the primary reference concept is satisfying the demands of the supply chain. (See Figure 7.3.)

It becomes easy to see how drill-down metrics network back to the main objectives of quality and productivity.

MOBILE METRICS

Mobile metrics! People on the move need to have their information on the run, especially travelers. The push method of delivery may be the most useful for getting critical information to an individual. Although the popular press advertisers are hyping mobile BI as though you cannot run a business without it, much thought should be given to this media. It is probably best to build out the platform first and keep the mobile ideas as a "nice to have" feature when time and money allow for its development.

On the other hand, from practical experience taking scorecard data and chunking it into bite-size *quick response* (QR), codes can communicate more information than a graphic. Translating the data into a QR code is transportable and can be printed to a PowerPoint slide for easy transfer to mobile devices, by scanning the code right from the screen by a group of people in a meeting, or e-mailed and shared. While QR codes may not seem an elegant means of delivery, it is fast and gets the job done at virtually little or no cost.

Encoding data types are many. One may therefore encode a link to a website location where the metrics are located for viewing (Figure 7.4).

JMP JOURNALS

Quite possibly the best way toward a presentation solution is to be able to share or make available a library of JMP JSL scripts available across the entire enterprise. The BI Competency Center keeps responsibility for maintaining the micro-data warehouse, and users simply run the script whenever they need a fresh set of metrics. Training the user community to start JMP on their workstation, open a script, and run it is a minimalistic task.

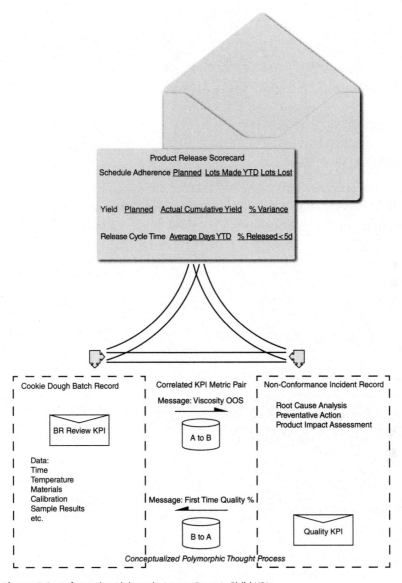

Figure 7.3 Information Linkage between Parent–Child KPIs

Figure 7.4 Quick Response Code

The visuals generated by JMP can also be saved in several formats in JMP such as to a journal window or file, or an html format. And lastly, users may find it perfectly acceptable to pick up a set of metrics from their local area network printer.

7.3 DIY, BUT LEAVE THE POOR BI PERSON ALONE!

KEEP THE DATA CURRENT—ALLOW ACCESS BY OTHERS

Although the statement "Do it yourself" (DIY) is tongue in cheek, many people do prefer to have access to the scripts for running the metrics on their own time. Assuming that the data virtualization server maintains data currency, this delivery concept might work best for people who are more statistically knowledgeable and have skills and training in the use of the JMP software.

As the CONNECTIONS platform grows and matures with a wide inventory of JMP scripts, these can be made easily available to the user community if organized in a meaningful way. Intuitively, they can be grouped by sets into specific knowledge asset groups. An easy to code (i.e., less than 30 lines) JMP window user interface can provide a list of available scripts with checkboxes by each for selection by the end user. Given the number of options available when coding up a script or run-time options, one efficient way to maintain organization over the scripts is to include them either in a data virtualized table or simply in a JMP table. Typically, a record in the table would contain the file name of the script, a title or description field, a path to the file name, and any other associated fields that might be relevant to a script such as whether the script has user interface dialogs for user input or whether tables opened by a script should be invisible. When the JMP window user interface starts, it can read in the table using the script title field for the checkbox line items. With the checkboxes, the user can select to run one or more scripts in one session. See Appendix C for a coding example. The actual JMP table and execution of the graphical user interface window follows in Figure 7.5.

The example in Appendix C utilizes the JMP Schedule function to queue up the scripts for execution where each runs in its own context. With the Schedule function, it is not possible to create multiple threads, most likely because the JMP script interpreter does not support or allow multiple threads of execution to exist within the context of a single process. No multithreaded support means the Scheduler does not lend itself to concurrent execution. A case where the inability to run or call a function multiple times to run in parallel might be evident to the person writing a JMP script is in calling the Schedule function within a iteration statement (i.e., a for loop) to start a multitude of different scripts at different start times. If it were concurrent, multiple schedulers would appear. But in fact, once the Scheduler is running, a secondary call does not add another Schedule instance, nor does it add the event to a Schedule process that is already running. When JMP.exe starts, a process is created. If a script is opened, the JMP interpreter can only do one thing at a time. It cannot perform multiple tasks in parallel. There are only a few operations in JMP that are multithreaded, such as higher-end analytics, sorting, and multicolumn distributions.

Later and very cleverly, if one wanted to build more smarts into script Regional Marketing Analysis.jsl, that script could query its own record to determine if it should display a User Interface (UI) Required dialog box for taking input, such as taking input for a date range prior to running the script. If the field indicates no UI Required, the script would run with the default values already coded into the script.

7.4 ADVANCED PRESENTATION METHOD

ADVANCED VISUALIZATION

In the world of science fiction, advance concepts like the multi-dimensional gaming board idea could be applied to the presentation of metrics. These ideas were known as Cubic Chess or in the movie series

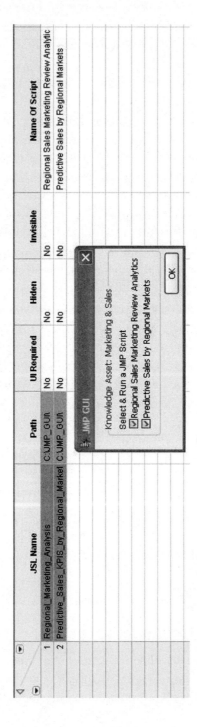

Figure 7.5 JMP GUI Window with JMP Table

Star Trek as the tri-dimensional or 3D chess game. To see them play gives one the impression that these guys must be highly intelligent to figure out all the optimal moves.

While there does not appear to be any multidimensional spreadsheet applications available, there are data sets that could be visualized in a scatter plot 3D manner on many levels or plains. The only application that comes to mind are computer-aided design (CAD) applications that utilize layers and overlays for people like civil engineers, who may be maintaining the facilities and physical plant of a municipality, or even mechanical engineers designing new aircraft.

In essence, large managed projects or enterprise business process schedules with people assigned to tasks or being moved around for optimal labor utilization is a multidimensional problem. Typically, project managers have a one-dimensional view of the world with Gantt charts and tools of their trade. Whether it is a project or a manufacturing setting, production is always planned ahead of time in the near future and tracked. Using the data from production plans in a novel way would help in getting people to the right task at the right time.

For example, a large manufacturer has many jobs taking place in many buildings whereby the production cycles have definitive starting and ending times. Using JMP to data mine from the production planning schedules for each building could be represented in a visual metric similar to a Gantt chart. However, rather than trying to see the enterprise production schedule in one large graphic, it would be better to produce a metric for each building. Once the metric graphic is generated for each building, the best way to put the visual together would be the old acetate overhead projector method. These were known as transparencies that could be printed and overlaid on one another for analysis. This same method could be achieved by utilizing the JMP output graphics in another piece of software called GNU Image Manipulation Program (GIMP) [2]. This software has a feature that graphic artists used to call *group layering*. One could take the JMP graphic image for each building and, with the GIMP tranparency layer, visualize the various production schedules multidimensionally for a period of time and see where there are gaps and overlaps, or where one job ends and another one immediately starts as a way of anticipating where workers need to go. 3D graphics can become a very powerful presentation method even though additional work is involved to superimpose the various layers against one another. Other graphics designers and illustrators, especially those making scientific illustrations for journal articles, may use software such as Inkscape [4] or Blender [1] among many other software packages that are available for photorealistic rendering. Rather than try to illustrate the concept with a graphic, it is most beneficial to say that JMP Pro has a mapping feature that is easily found in their documentation. For advanced 2D and 3D visualization, many companies may already find they have the basic visual background graphics for office building complexes, shop floor plans, or utilities in CAD drawing formats. With data from enterprise resource planning (ERP), manufacturing execution system (MES), supervisory control and data acquisition (SCADA), and other process control systems (PCS) potentially available through data virtualization and ultimately as JMP input, one can start to see many use cases for mapping data onto the graphic by way of JMP scripting and delivering a spectacular added value in support of business operations. Figure 7.6 is the basic fundamental office temperature mapping study conducted at SAS.

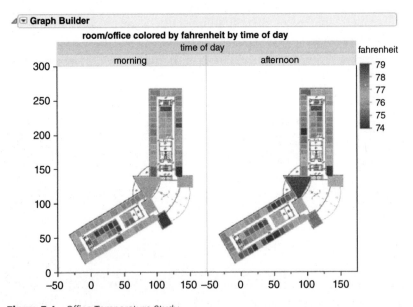

Figure 7.6 Office Temperature Study

In support of advanced 3D visualization and possible use cases, a whitepaper from the European Mathematical Information Service is available titled, "Use Cases and Concepts for 3D Visualisation in Manufacturing." [11] In order to implement 3D visualization support, information from different data sources is required and thus another case for JMP CONNECTIONS data virtualization. Authors Bernhard Wolf, Gerald, Mofor and Jochen Rode state the following:

> However, apart from the 3D geometric data other data is required and needs to be mapped to the visualization. These data can be classified in four categories, namely: master data (i.e., data valid for an extended period of time), transactional data (i.e., data relevant for a shorter time frame and a particular business transaction), real-time data (i.e., current data from the manufacturing process), and KPI data (i.e., key performance indicators that aggregate other data) [11].

Their concepts of visualization are Resource Status Visualization, Routing Visualization, Localization Visualization, and Production Progress Visualization, but such concepts may not necessarily map one-to-one to your own use cases. Some creativity is required when developing advanced designs. Along with current data, historical data may be as relevant for display for possible data overlays. For example, on a 3D shop floor graphic, data may include personnel information, nonconformances, alarms, or real-time data from historian systems to name a few. The four categories of data in the context of a manufacturing site are nicely expanded upon by the authors as follows:

> *Master data* relevant for implementing the discussed scenarios include the plant layout (locations, resources), the plant personnel (skills), the process (routings), the bill of material (BOM) structure, tools, and maintenance documents. The systems of record for these types of master data are typically ERP systems and MES [11].
>
> *Transactional data* include production or maintenance orders and confirmations. Transactional data are typically managed in MES and ERP systems [11].

Figure 7.7 Chocolate velvet anyone?

Real-time data include process and resource information like machine status (e.g., available, idle, working, tool break, in repair), current yield, scrap, and rework quantity, operating hours, process parameters (e.g., tank fill level or temperature), exceptions (e.g., unplanned downtimes, breakdowns), and WIP locations. Real-time data originate either from the shop floor (machine data) or from the MES (information derived from technical data) [11].

KPI data provide meaningful feedback about the performance of a production process and include such KPIs as OEE (e.g., Overall Equipment Effectiveness), quality data, etc. KPI data is typically generated and processed by the MES [11].

If your company or organization has accomplished this level of maturity both in data-refined metrics and visual presentation, then it is time for a pat on the back. Roll out the corporate cake! (See Figure 7.7.)

CHAPTER 8

In Closing (As-Built)

THE PREDICTIVE, DESCRIPTIVE, AND PRESCRIPTIVE ACUMINOUS BUSINESS

It has been said, "You cannot not manage what you cannot measure,"[1] implying the use of metrics is an absolute.

> I often say that when you can measure what you are speaking about, and express it in numbers, you know something about it; but when you cannot express it in numbers, your knowledge is of a meagre and unsatisfactory kind; it may be the beginning of knowledge, but you have scarcely, in your thoughts, advanced to the stage of science, whatever the matter may be [33].[2] (Lecture on "Electrical Units of Measurement" (3 May 1883), published in *Popular Lectures*, Vol. I, p. 7. See Figure 8.1 and http://en.wikiquote.org/wiki/File:Hubert_von_Herkomer03.jpg).

Thus, when a strategic objective has been cast, the formulation of the strategy has a clear set of objectives for execution. Critical success factors are then linked to well-chosen performance metrics, so-called key performance indicators. Corporate performance management is in union with and intersects with decision process improvement. If operational performance was perfect, there would be no need for decisions to make adjustments by management. In fact, metrics alone do not guarantee optimal decisions. The decision maker also may not have the perfect expertise and skills through education or experience to make the best choice.

The decisions being made now, after the fact that an enterprise deploys the model described here as the JMP CONNECTIONS platform, will be recognizably incremental as parts or pieces roll out. Given time to maturity, components rolled in the aggregate across an enterprise as capability and maturity proliferates should embolden decision makers.

---

[1] A vitiate paraphase of modified variations, perhaps quoted by many such as Deming, Hewlett, Druker, and Peters as a management adage, traced back to Lord Kelvin.
[2] William Thomson (June 26, 1824 December 17, 1907), First Baron Kelvin, often referred to simply as Lord Kelvin, was a Scottish physicist.

Figure 8.1 Public Domain: William Thomson Oil Painting

Better decisions mean a smoother running operation, best practice control over plans and budgets, exceeding customer expectations, and ultimately hitting performance targets to realize better profits and return on the business investment. More than just software, hardware, and numbers, the model is intended to professionally develop the human resources, get everyone involved, and give people a wonderful experience at work.

Supplemental to metrics are two precepts derived from semantic knowledge assets for decision process improvement. Knowledge acquisition involves on the part of the decision maker complex cognitive processes: perception, learning, communication, association, and reasoning. The word *knowledge* is also used to mean the confident understanding of the subject with the ability to use it for a specific purpose. Identifying a good balance of critical success factors should also include the yield from incorporating the use of knowledge assets. A deeper meaning to the metrics and concepts, highly relevant but not necessarily more facts and clarity of the bigger picture, will lead to better decisions and less variation over the course and real-time stratagem execution.

The JMP CONNECTIONS platform can be viewed as its own ecosystem for business intelligence activities. Given the holistic purpose of corporate resilience and sustainability in a data-intensive industry such as biopharmaceuticals, petrochemicals, or any manufacturing setting for that matter, access to data and information enables companies to understand and streamline their operating and business processes. Getting the right information to the right people at the right time is critical for understanding and improving existing processes within an organization. Unfortunately, so many firms fail to leverage their information assets for better decisions because they mismanage it, or they are not managing it at all. Prerequisites for building the JMP CONNECTIONS solution requires understanding an organization's data and information landscape. But more than anything else, a subject matter expert must be intimate with the very foundation of creating a metric which actually dictates the specification of the platform and the profile and semantics of the micro-data warehouse. Thus, the learning curve for utilizing information assets is exactly why it has been suggested to start out this project small as a bottom-up approach. A low investment for development makes sense when economic conditions are less than ideal. As a pilot project, it can earn its reputation, grow laterally across other organizations, and eventually scale up on the grounds of achieving new levels of capability; and human resources will slowly gain new competency in the process.

From the perspective of a CEO in a large company, the expectation is that manufacturing is going to happen regardless of the operational business metrics and the competency center's ability to report business intelligence. Ultimately, the biggest concern is resources and people. So sooner or later the question comes down to how many FTEs can be saved or reduced in the enterprise. Data virtualization with JMP Pro as the front end is a shining case where it can be concretely demonstrated how FTE savings is achieved. The As-Built or design fabrication of the JMP CONNECTIONS model, the specification coming out of data virtualization for consolidating knowledge assets, reducing spreadsheet usage, and reporting redundancies, yields the kind of data showing a reduction of FTEs that almost every owner or CEO is looking for to achieve resounding business success.

As the building of knowledge assets takes place, the linkages between the operational metrics and the dependencies in this network of links becomes clear. The metric concepts of safety, quality, productivity, and cost and the relationships of measuring and monitoring processes, people, and equipment clearly blend into rolling throughput yields (aka, first time quality). FTQ is an action of abridging and then combining various multifactor productivity (i.e., conceptual integration) that ultimately is reflected as FTE KPIs, a part of corporate performance management. Metrics bring out the best in people. If you need proof of this fact, just ask yourself why baseball fanatics cite and track statistics on the records of players and teams. Beating a record happens to be a very cognitive, fulfilling need for players, fans, and organizations. Measuring the productivity of people is very easily done. Measuring the productivity of a team is not the aggregate of the productivity of individuals. A team is measured on progress and results. A team of high performers may not produce good team productivity. Team productivity or collaborative effectiveness is altogether another type of metric called "Cognitive-Based Metrics to Evaluate Collaboration Effectiveness" [24]. A treatment of the subject matter can be found by research from Noble and Letsky at http://www .au.af.mil/au/awc/awcgate/navy/onr_metrics_on_collab.pdf as well as articles on metrics-based project governance where teamwork and collaborative initiatives are pillars driving profitability in large enterprises.

It may take a very large team to manufacture a product or perform business tasks in an organization which is representative within the framework of FTEs. Ongoing task-based teams are very different than a team working on a project. A project has a starting point and a definitive end. A project has a vision and an execution path where variability can happen when the execution wanders off the vision, requiring realignment through the journey. The manufacturing or business team operates within the parameters of standard operating procedures (SOPs) and standard work instructions (SWIs) along with concrete data that is the essence of this entire discussion. No company can live without these two types of distinct team concepts. The project to build a manufacturing facility eventually will be turned over to operations. When this turnover happens, it may be the best opportunity to build out the knowledge assets and metrics that will be used over the life cycle of the business to ultimately leverage the firm's capital because it offers the highest potential for increasing the average rate of return.

From As-Is to As-Built, the design fabrication of the JMP CONNEC-TIONS model, from Capability Levels 0, 1, 2, 3 and beyond to advanced analytic metrics, employs data assets heretofore underutilized.

> * PREDICTIVE (Forecasting)
> * DESCRIPTIVE (Business Intelligence and Data Mining)
> * PRESCRIPTIVE (Modeling, Optimization, and Simulation)

Appendix G is a storyline look at a pathway up the Figure 1.3 capability curve and the overlay where levels intersect in the capability maturity design space for As-Built advanced analytical metrics.

A mature predictive, descriptive, and prescriptive business assures its own future sustainability, business process control in execution, opportunities, and profitability.

Glossary

AJAX A group of interrelated web development techniques used on the client side to create asynchronous web applications.

As-Built May refer to a field survey, construction drawing, 3D model, or other descriptive representation of an engineered project or a design. Derived from usage of the adjective *as-built*.

ASD Adjustable speed drive.

BB A black box (BB) in the context of engineering or science conceptually is a device, system, or object that can be viewed in terms of its input and output without any knowledge of its internal workings.

BDG Box description graphics.

BDL Box description language.

BI Business intelligence.

BRF BI risk factor.

BSM Business service management.

CAPEX Capital expenditure.

CB A clear box (CB) can be thought of as the opposite of a black box and is a system where the inner components or logic are available for inspection.

CMVC Configuration Management Version Control.

COBOL COmmon Business-Oriented Language.

CPI A process is a set of steps to accomplish a defined purpose or produce a defined product or service. Continuous process improvement is the set of ongoing systems engineering and management activities used to select, tailor, implement, and assess the processes used to achieve an organization's business goals. Continuous improvement is recognized as a component of modern quality management [6].

CPV Continued process verification (CPV) is the activity that provides ongoing verification of the performance of a manufacturing process.

Cron   Cron is driven by a crontab (cron table) file, a configuration file that specifies shell commands to run periodically on a given schedule.

Crontabs   A configuration table for running scheduled cron jobs.

Cygwin   NIX-like environment for Windows.

Daemon   Daemon is a computer program that runs as a background process, rather than being under the direct control of an interactive user.

DOS   Disk operating system.

DVCS   Distributed Version Control System.

DVS   Data virtualization server.

Emacs   Extraordinarily powerful text editor.

ERP   Enterprise resource planning.

EWMA   Exponentially weighted moving average.

FTE   Full-time equivalent.

FTQ   First-time quality.

GUID   Globally unique identifier.

HVAC   Heating, ventilation, and air conditioning.

INSERT   INSERT is a SQL database construct for writing a record to a database.

IT   Information technology.

JMP   Pronounced "jump," John's MacIntosh Program.

JOIN   JOIN is a SQL database construct for accessing data from multiple tables.

JSON   (JavaScript Object Notation) is a lightweight data-interchange format.

KPI   Key performance indicator.

LAMP   Linux Apache MySql PHP.

LCC   Life-cycle costs.

LCL   Lower control limit.

MES   Manufacturing execution system.

MSE   Mean square error.

MTBF   Mean time between failures.

MySql   MySql is an open source relational database system.

NEMA   National Electrical Manufacturers Association.

NIX   Short acronym for Unix/Linux operating systems.

ODBC   Open database connectivity.

OEE   Overall equipment effectiveness.

OLAP   On-line analytical process.

OLE   Object linking and embedding.

Ontology   In theory, an ontology is a "formal, explicit specification of a shared conceptualization."

PAT   Process analytical technology.

PCS   Process control systems.

Perl   Perl is a high-level programming language; though not an official acronym, there are various backronyms in use such as Practical Extraction and Reporting Language.

PHP   PHP hypertext preprocessor.

PLC   Programmable Logic Controller.

POS   Point of sale.

QR   Quick response.

RDF   Resource Description Framework.

RFT   Right first time.

RMSE   Root mean square error.

SAMBA   Samba is an open source/free software suite that provides seamless file and print services to SMB/CIFS clients.

SAP   German software corporation that makes enterprise software to manage business operations.

SAS   (Pronounced "sass," originally Statistical Analysis System) is an integrated system of software products provided by SAS Institute Inc.

SCADA   Supervisory Control and Data Acquisition.

SDLC   Software development life cycle.

Semantic Of or pertaining to meaning or arising from the different meanings of words or other symbols.

SM State machine (SM) is a concept used in the design of computer programs or digital logic.

SME Subject matter expert.

SOA Service-oriented architecture.

SOH SPARQL Over HTTP.

SOP Standard operating procedure.

SPARQL A recursive acronym for SPARQL Protocol and RDF Query Language and is an RDF query language.

SPC Statistical process control.

SQL Structured Query Language.

SWI Standard work instructions.

TPM Total productive maintenance.

UCL Upper control limit.

UML Unified Modeling Language.

VB Visual Basic.

VIEW A VIEW consists of a stored query accessible as a virtual table in a relational database.

VSD Variable-speed drive.

WAMP Windows Apache MySql PHP.

WFI Water for injection.

XML Extensible Markup Language (XML) is a markup language that defines a set of rules for encoding documents in a format that is both human-readable and machine-readable.

Server-Side PHP Code

```php
<?php                                                              1
$dbhost = "localhost";                                             2
$dbuser = "jwubbel";                                               3
$dbpass = "sonora3010";                                            4
$dbname = "micro_data_warehouse";                                  5
                                                                   6
        //Connect to MySQL Server                                  7
$con = mysql_connect($dbhost, $dbuser, $dbpass);                   8
                                                                   9
        //Select Database                                         10
mysql_select_db($dbname) or die(mysql_error());                   11
                                                                  12
        // Retrieve data from Query String                        13
$results = json_decode($_GET['json'], true);                      14
.                                                                 15
.                                                                 16
.                                                                 17
.                                                                 18
.                                                                 19
$rs = mysql_query("INSERT_INTO_oee_stamp_data_(press_date)_       20
    VALUES('$Stamp_Press_Date')") or die (mysql_error());
                                                                  21
if ($rs) {                                                        22
    echo "TRUE";                                                  23
}                                                                 24
else {                                                            25
    echo "Database_Error_on_record_insertion!";                  26
}                                                                 27
                                                                  28
mysql_close($con);                                                29
                                                                  30
?>                                                                31
```

JMP JSL Time Constant Learning Curve Script

```
// open the database and initialize the table with columns        1
   from the die_cut_stamp_oee view
dt = Open Database("DSN=Heavy_Metal_Metrics;UID=jwubbel;PWD=   2
   geu33b;SERVER=localhost;DATABASE=micro_data_warehouse;PORT
   =3306;", "SELECT_*_FROM_DIE_CUT_STAMP_OEE_ORDER_BY_Date_
   ASC", "PLANT_29_OEE_SUPER_STAMPER_CONTROL_CHART");
                                                                  3
// add in the column for sequencing required by the Time          4
   Constant Learning Curve algorithm
dc_seq = dt << Add Multiple Columns( "seq", 1,                   5
   "Before_First", numeric, continuous, best, 3 );
                                                                  6
// initial the seq column with row numbers                        7
For Each Row(seq=Row());                                          8
                                                                  9
// count total number of rows in the current table               10
iRowCnt = N Row(dt);                                             11
                                                                  12
// add new columns                                               13
                                                                  14
// create new columns for facilitating the newton-gaussian       15
   non-linear regression calculations
dc_nc = dt<<NewColumn("Errors",numeric,best);                   16
dc_nc << Set Modeling Type("Continuous");                       17
                                                                  18
dc_lp = dt<<NewColumn("Estimated_OEE",numeric,best);            19
dc_lp << Set Modeling Type("Continuous");                       20
                                                                  21
// set up script to recalculate the learning curve starting      22
   values for the "Estimated OEE" parameters
dc_lc = dt<<NewColumn("x-formula",numeric,best);                23
dc_lc << Set Modeling Type("Continuous");                       24
                                                                  25
// set the Time Constant Learning Curve formula for the          26
   column "Estimated OEE"
dc_lc << Add Column Properties(                                  27
     Formula(                                                    28
          Parameter(                                             29
               {Yc = 57.6, Yf = 10, t =                          30
          20},                                                   31
               Yc + Yf *(1 - Exp(-seq/t))                        32
          )                                                      33
     )                                                           34
);                                                              35
```

```
// Define script to run Nonlinear iterations                      37
dt << New Script(                                                 38
        "Nonlinear",                                             39
        Nonlinear(                                               40
            Y( :OEE ),                                           41
            X( :x-formula ),                                     42
            Iteration Limit( 200 ),                              43
            Newton,                                              44
            Finish                                               45
        )                                                        46
    );                                                           47
                                                                 48
// because we likely will be appending new cycle data for        49
    each batch the starting values for computing Nonlinear on
    the Estimated OEE column
// need to be recalculated each time. Thus, this eliminated       50
    the need to do this manually everytime.
obj =   Nonlinear(                                                51
                    Y( :OEE ),                                   52
                    X( :Name( "x-formula" ) ),                   53
                    Iteration Limit( 200 ),                      54
                    Newton,                                      55
                    Finish                                       56
                );                                               57
                                                                 58
G = obj << Get Estimates;  // pull the 3 values out of the        59
    function after convergence
                                                                 60
// use the values in array G for use in setting up the           61
    column properties for the Estimate OEE
                                                                 62
// set the formula for the column "Errors"                       63
dc_nc << Add Column Properties                                   64
        (Formula(                                                65
                OEE - Estimated OEE                              66
                )                                                67
        );                                                       68
                                                                 69
// set the Time Constant Learning Curve formula for the          70
    column "Estimated OEE",
// substitute in new parameters that were generated by the       71
    Nonlinear call above.
dc_lp << Add Column Properties(                                  72
        Formula(                                                 73
                Parameter(                                       74
                        {Yc = G[1], Yf = G[2], t =               75
                G[3]},                                           76
```

```
                              Yc + Yf *(1 - Exp(-seq/t))         77
               )                                                  78
          )                                                       79
);                                                                80
                                                                  81
// Define script to run Nonlinear iterations                      82
dt << New Script(                                                 83
               "Nonlinear",                                       84
               Nonlinear(                                         85
                    Y( :OEE ),                                    86
                    X( :Estimated OEE ),                          87
                    Iteration Limit( 200 ),                       88
                    Newton,                                       89
                    Finish                                        90
               )                                                  91
          );                                                      92
                                                                  93
// define script to generate the control chart for the errors.   94
dt << New Script(                                                 95
               "PLANT_29_OEE_SUPER_STAMPER_CONTROL_CHART",        96
               Control Chart(                                     97
                    Sample Label( :Date ),                        98
                    KSigma( 3 ),                                  99
                    Weight( 0.2 ),                                100
                    Chart Col( :Errors, EWMA ),                   101
                    title("Total_Productive_Maintenance_-_        102
                        OEE_SUPER_STAMPER_-_029STAMP_CORP"),
                    SendToReport(                                 103
                    Dispatch(                                     104
                         {"EWMA_of_Errors"},                      105
                         "2",                                     106
                         ScaleBox,                                107
                         {Show Major Grid( 1 ), Show              108
                             Minor Ticks( 0 )}
                         ),                                       109
                    Dispatch(                                     110
                         {"EWMA_of_Errors"},                      111
                         "1",                                     112
                         ScaleBox,                                113
                         {Min( 0.5 ), Max( iRowCnt+1 ),           114
                             Inc( 1 ),
                         Minor Ticks( 0 ), Show Major             115
                             Grid( 1 ), Show Minor
                             Grid( 0 ), Rotated
                             Labels( 1 )}
                         ),                                       116
```

```
                        Dispatch(                                117
                                {"EWMA_of_Errors"},              118
                                "Moving_Average",               119
                                FrameBox,                        120
                                {Frame Size( 1097, 567 ),        121
                                    Marker Size( 2 )}
                                )                                122
                        )                                        123
                )                                                124
        );                                                       125
                                                                 126
// automatically run and open the control chart so user does     127
    not have to do so
dt << Control Chart(                                             128
                        Sample Label( :Date ),                   129
                        KSigma( 3 ),                             130
                        Weight( 0.2 ),                           131
                        Chart Col( :Errors, EWMA ),              132
                        title("Total_Productive_Maintenance_-_    133
                            OEE_SUPER_STAMPER_-_029STAMP_CORP"),
                        SendToReport(                            134
                        Dispatch(                                135
                                {"EWMA_of_Errors"},              136
                                "2",                             137
                                ScaleBox,                         138
                                {Show Major Grid( 1 ), Show       139
                                    Minor Ticks( 0 )}
                                ),                               140
                        Dispatch(                                141
                                {"EWMA_of_Errors"},              142
                                "1",                             143
                                ScaleBox,                         144
                                {Min( 0.5 ), Max( iRowCnt+1 ),    145
                                    Inc( 1 ),
                                Minor Ticks( 0 ), Show Major      146
                                    Grid( 1 ), Show Minor
                                    Grid( 0 ), Rotated
                                    Labels( 1 )}
                                ),                               147
                        Dispatch(                                148
                                {"EWMA_of_Errors"},              149
                                "Moving_Average",               150
                                FrameBox,                        151
                                {Frame Size( 1097, 567 ),        152
                                    Marker Size( 2 )}
                                )                                153
                        )                                        154
                );                                               155
```

JMP GUI User Interface Code Example

```
Names Default To Here(1);                                              1
// Load the table containing the scripts and script names              2
script_dt = Open("C:\JMP_GUI\JMP_GUI.jmp");                            3
// get a count of how many rows are in the table for later             4
   reference
iRowCnt = N Row(script_dt);                                            5
Show(iRowCnt);                                                         6
// get the values from the columns followed by inserting them          7
   into a list
lst_of_jsl_names = column(script_dt,"Name_Of_Script") <<              8
   GetAsMatrix();
lst_of_script_filenames = column(script_dt,"JSL_Name") <<             9
   GetAsMatrix();
lst_of_script_path = column(script_dt,"Path") << GetAsMatrix();       10
lst_of_rows = list();                                                 11
lst_of_rows_selected = list();                                        12
// put the names of the scripts into a list                           13
rCnt = 0;                                                             14
for (rCnt = 1, rCnt < iRowCnt + 1, rCnt++,                           15
        InsertInto(lst_of_rows,lst_of_jsl_names[rCnt]);               16
);                                                                   17
// Create a modal window to display the scripts for user              18
   selection
nw = New Window( "JMP_GUI", <<modal(),                               19
        Show Menu( false ),                                           20
        Suppress AutoHide,                                           21
        Show Toolbars( false ),                                       22
        Panel Box( "Knowledge_Asset:_Marketing_&_Sales",            23
            Text Box( "Select_&_Run_a_JMP_Script" ),                 24
            ckb = Check Box( lst_of_rows )  // enumerated            25
                list of check boxes to display
            )                                                        26
);                                                                   27
// get the scripts that were selected by the user and put them        28
   into a list
for (iCnt = 1, iCnt < iRowCnt + 1, iCnt++,                           29
        InsertInto(lst_of_rows_selected, ckb << Get(iCnt));          30
);                                                                   31
iStartTimeIn = 5; // count down time in seconds to start             32
   executing the first event
                                                                     33
// It should be noted here that multiple calls to function            34
   Schedule
// will not result in starting multiple threads.                     35
// Therefore, the only way to stack up events in the queue for        36
   the
```

```
// Scheduler is to pack them all into the call prior to          37
   executing the function.
// We use a programming trick here that essentially is self      38
   modifying code.
// So, to overcome this problem, we build the function call      39
   into a string variable,
// write or save the variable data to a jsl file and then        40
   turn around to Include it
// into the current script. It runs each script in the order     41
   in which they were
// stuffed into function call parameters.                        42
                                                                 43
// EXAMPLE:                                                       44
/*                                                               45
Schedule(5,                                                      46
     Include("C:\JMP_GUI\Regional_Marketing_Analysis.JSL", <<    47
        New Context);
        Include("C:\JMP_GUI\                                     48
           Predictive_Sales_KPIS_by_Regional_Markets.JSL", <<
           New Context);
);                                                               49
*/                                                               50
// Next we define constants                                      51
strSchedule = "Schedule(";                                       52
strIRunner = Char(iStartTimeIn);                                 53
strCommaSpace = ",_";                                            54
strInclude = "Include(";                                         55
strQuote = "\!"";                                                56
strParenSemi_=_");";                                             57
strNewContext_=_", <<New Context";                               58
strNewLine_=_"\!N";                                              59
//_commence_building_the_string_that_becomes_our_function_call   60
strSchedule_||_=_strIRunner;                                     61
strSchedule_||_=_strCommaSpace;                                  62
                                                                 63
for_(iCntFE_=_1, _iCntFE_<_iRowCnter_+_1, _iCntFE++,             64
___if_(lst_of_rows_selected[iCntFE] _>_0,                        65
_____str_ScriptPathFileName_=_lst_of_script_path[iCntFE];       66
_____str_ScriptPathFileName_||_=_lst_of_script_filenames        67
   [iCntFE];
_____str_ScriptPathFileName_||_=_".JSL";                        68
                                                                 69
_____strSchedule_||_=_strNewLine;                               70
_____strSchedule_||_=_strInclude;                               71
_____strSchedule_||_=_strQuote;                                 72
_____strSchedule_||_=_str_ScriptPathFileName;                   73
```

```
_____strSchedule_||=_strQuote;                                    74
_____strSchedule_||=_strNewContext;                               75
_____strSchedule_||=_strParenSemi;                                76
___);                                                              77
);                                                                 78
strSchedule_||=_strParenSemi;                                      79
                                                                   80
Save_Text_File(_"C:\JMP_GUI\Schedule.jsl",_strSchedule);           81
Wait(1);_//_give_the_file_system_a_second_to_do_the_write_to_      82
   disk
//_Execute_the_Scheduler                                           83
Include("C:\JMP_GUI\Schedule.jsl", _<<New_Context);                84
```

Resource Description Framework File Example

```
<rdf:RDF                                                              1
    xmlns:rdf="http://www.w3.org/1999/02/22-rdf-syntax-ns#"          2
    xmlns:rdfs="http://www.w3.org/2000/01/rdf-schema#"               3
    xmlns:owl="http://www.w3.org/2002/07/owl#"                       4
    xmlns:uo="http://purl.obolibrary.org/obo/uo.owl"                 5
    xmlns:n="http://www.nist.gov/units/"                             6
    xmlns:xsd="http://www.w3.org/2001/XMLSchema#"                    7
    xmlns:dc="http://purl.org/dc/elements/1.1/"                      8
    xmlns:ns1="http://cookie/">                                      9
    xmlns:ns2="http://cookie_mfg/dough_dept#">                      10
    xmlns:ns3="http://cookie_metrics/kitchen_depart#">              11
    xmlns:ns4="http://cookie_recipe/materials_dept#">               12
                                                                    13
    <rdf:Description rdf:about="http://cookie_mfg/recipe#           14
        Alaskan_Cowboy_Cookies">
        <ns1:Dessert>A Cookie Popular In Alaska</ns1:Dessert>       15
        <ns1:Ingredients rdf:resource="http://cookie_recipe/       16
            material#Ingredients"/>
    </rdf:Description>                                              17
                                                                    18
    <rdf:Description rdf:about="http://cookie_recipe/material       19
        #Ingredients">
        <ns1:Flour>All Purpose Flour</ns1:Flour>                   20
        <ns1:Baking_Soda>Baking Soda</ns1:Baking_Soda>             21
        <ns1:Baking_Powder>Baking Powder</ns1:Baking_Powder>       22
        <ns1:Salt>Salt</ns1:Salt>                                  23
        <ns1:Butter>Unsalted Butter</ns1:Butter>                   24
        <ns1:Sugar>Sugar</ns1:Sugar>                               25
        <ns1:Brown_Sugar>Dark Brown Sugar</ns1:Brown_Sugar>        26
        <ns1:Eggs>Eggs</ns1:Eggs>                                  27
        <ns1:Vanilla>Vanilla Extract</ns1:Vanilla>                 28
        <ns1:Oats>Old Fashion Oats</ns1:Oats>                      29
        <ns1:Chocolate_Chips>semisweet chocolate chips</           30
            ns1:Chocolate_Chips>
    </rdf:Description>                                              31
                                                                    32
    <rdf:Description rdf:about="http://cookie/Contains#            33
        Dry_Ingredients">
        <ns1:Contains>All Purpose Flour</ns1:Contains>             34
        <ns1:Contains>Baking Soda</ns1:Contains>                   35
        <ns1:Contains>Baking Powder</ns1:Contains>                 36
        <ns1:Contains>Salt</ns1:Contains>                          37
    </rdf:Description>                                              38
                                                                    39
    <rdf:Description rdf:about="http://cookie/Contains#            40
        Wet_Ingredients">
```

```
    <ns1:Contains>Unsalted Butter</ns1:Contains>              41
    <ns1:Contains>Sugar</ns1:Contains>                        42
    <ns1:Brown_Sugar>Dark Brown Sugar</ns1:Brown_Sugar>       43
    <ns1:Eggs>Eggs</ns1:Eggs>                                 44
    <ns1:Vanilla>Vanilla Extract</ns1:Vanilla>                45
  </rdf:Description>                                          46
                                                              47

<rdf:Description rdf:about="http://cookie/Contains#          48
  AddIn_Ingredients">
    <ns1:Contains>Old Fashion Oats</ns1:Contains>             49
    <ns1:Contains>semisweet chocolate chips</ns1:Contains>   50
  </rdf:Description>                                          51
                                                              52

<rdf:Description rdf:about="http://cookie_mfg/batch#        53
  CM6070">
    <ns1:Part_Number>450189</ns1:Part_Number>                 54
    <ns1:Assemblage_Date>23Nov2013</ns1:Assemblage_Date>      55
    <ns1:Name_Of_Cookie>Alaskan Cowboy Cookies</              56
      ns1:Name_Of_Cookie>
    <ns1:Dry_Ingredients rdf:resource="http://cookie/        57
      Contains#Dry_Ingredients"/>
    <ns1:Wet_Ingredients rdf:resource="http://cookie/        58
      Contains#Wet_Ingredients"/>
    <ns1:AddIn_Ingredients rdf:resource="http://cookie/      59
      Contains#AddIn_Ingredients"/>
    <ns1:Cookie_Metrics rdf:resource="http://cookie_         60
      metric/Batch#CM6070"/>
  </rdf:Description>                                          61
                                                              62
                                                              63

<rdf:Description rdf:about="http://cookie_metric/Batch#     64
  CM6070">
  <n:Flour rdf:parseType="Resource">                         65
  <rdf:Type>Unbleached Pastry Flour</rdf:Type>               66
  </n:Flour>                                                  67
                                                              68

  <n:Volume rdf:parseType="Resource">                        69
  <uo:is_unit_of>cup</uo:is_unit_of>                          70
  <rdf:Flour rdf:datatype="float">2</rdf:Flour>              71
  </n:Volume>                                                 72
                                                              73

  <n:Baking_Soda rdf:parseType="Resource">                   74
  <rdf:Type>Arm And Hammer</rdf:Type>                         75
  </n:Baking_Soda>                                            76
                                                              77

  <n:Volume rdf:parseType="Resource">                        78
  <uo:is_unit_of>teaspoon</uo:is_unit_of>                     79
```

```
<rdf:Baking_Soda rdf:datatype="float">1</        80
    rdf:Baking_Soda>
</n:Volume>                                        81
                                                   82
<n:Baking_Powder rdf:parseType="Resource">        83
<rdf:Type>Rumford</rdf:Type>                       84
</n:Baking_Powder>                                 85
                                                   86
<n:Volume rdf:parseType="Resource">               87
<uo:is_unit_of>teaspoon</uo:is_unit_of>            88
<rdf:Baking_Powder rdf:datatype="float">0.5</      89
    rdf:Baking_Powder>
</n:Volume>                                        90
                                                   91
<n:Salt rdf:parseType="Resource">                  92
<rdf:Type>Morton</rdf:Type>                        93
</n:Salt>                                          94
                                                   95
<n:Volume rdf:parseType="Resource">                96
<uo:is_unit_of>teaspoon</uo:is_unit_of>            97
<rdf:Salt rdf:datatype="float">0.5</rdf:Salt>      98
</n:Volume>                                        99
                                                   100
<n:Butter rdf:parseType="Resource">                101
<rdf:Type>Kraft</rdf:Type>                         102
</n:Butter>                                         103
                                                   104
<n:Volume rdf:parseType="Resource">                105
<uo:is_unit_of>cup</uo:is_unit_of>                 106
<rdf:Butter rdf:datatype="float">1</rdf:Butter>    107
</n:Volume>                                         108
                                                   109
<n:Sugar rdf:parseType="Resource">                 110
<rdf:Type>Domino</rdf:Type>                         111
</n:Sugar>                                          112
                                                   113
<n:Volume rdf:parseType="Resource">                114
<uo:is_unit_of>cup</uo:is_unit_of>                 115
<rdf:Sugar rdf:datatype="float">0.5</rdf:Sugar>    116
</n:Volume>                                         117
                                                   118
<n:Dark_Brown_Sugar rdf:parseType="Resource">      119
<rdf:Type>Domino</rdf:Type>                         120
</n:Dark_Brown_Sugar>                               121
                                                   122
<n:Volume rdf:parseType="Resource">                123
<uo:is_unit_of>cup</uo:is_unit_of>                 124
```

```
    <rdf:Dark_Brown_Sugar rdf:datatype="float">0.5</      125
      rdf:Dark_Brown_Sugar>
  </n:Volume>                                             126
                                                          127

  <n:Eggs rdf:parseType="Resource">                       128
  <rdf:Type>Organic</rdf:Type>                            129
  </n:Eggs>                                               130
                                                          131

  <n:Volume rdf:parseType="Resource">                     132
  <uo:is_unit_of>large</uo:is_unit_of>                    133
  <rdf:Eggs rdf:datatype="float">2</rdf:Eggs>             134
  </n:Volume>                                             135
                                                          136

  <n:Vanilla rdf:parseType="Resource">                    137
  <rdf:Type>McCormick</rdf:Type>                          138
  </n:Vanilla>                                            139
                                                          140

  <n:Volume rdf:parseType="Resource">                     141
  <uo:is_unit_of>teaspoon</uo:is_unit_of>                 142
  <rdf:Vanilla rdf:datatype="float">0.5</rdf:Vanilla>     143
  </n:Volume>                                             144
                                                          145

  <n:Oats rdf:parseType="Resource">                       146
  <rdf:Type>Honeyville</rdf:Type>                         147
  </n:Oats>                                               148
                                                          149

  <n:Volume rdf:parseType="Resource">                     150
  <uo:is_unit_of>cup</uo:is_unit_of>                      151
  <rdf:Oats rdf:datatype="float">2</rdf:Oats>             152
  </n:Volume>                                             153
                                                          154

  <n:Semi_Sweet_Chocolate_Chips rdf:parseType="Resource">  155
  <rdf:Type>Nestle</rdf:Type>                             156
  </n:Semi_Sweet_Chocolate_Chips>                         157
                                                          158

  <n:Volume rdf:parseType="Resource">                     159
  <uo:is_unit_of>cup</uo:is_unit_of>                      160
  <rdf:Semi_Sweet_Chocolate_Chips rdf:datatype="float">   161
    1.5</rdf:Semi_Sweet_Chocolate_Chips>
  </n:Volume>                                             162
                                                          163

</rdf:Description>                                        164
                                                          165
                                                          166
                                                          167
                                                          168
</rdf:RDF>                                                 169
```

Sample Hardware Requirements

-Configurable- HP Z800 Windows Workstation FF825AV

HP Z800 Workstation

Genuine Windows 7 Professional 64-bit (Not supported with RAM 1GB.)

HP Z800 1110W 89% Efficient Chassis

HP Z800 Localization Kit

Intel Xeon E5607 2.26 8MB/1066 4C CPU-1(LOWPWR)

Intel Xeon E5607 2.26 4MB/1066 QC CPU-2 (LOWPWR)(Must be same speed as Processor 1)

HP Air Cooling Solution (Must order Heatsink with this item.)

HP 2x Standard Heatsink Thermal Kit (Required if Air Cooling Thermal Kit selected and two processors are LOWPWR.)

NVIDIA Quadro 600 1.0GB Graphics

HP 16GB (8x2GB) DDR3-1333 ECC RAM (Supported only with Dual Processor.)

HP 250GB SATA 7200 1st HDD

HP 1000GB SATA 7200 2nd HDD

HP 16X DVD+-RW SuperMulti SATA 1st Drive

HP PS/2 Standard Keyboard

HP PS/2 Optical Scroll Mouse

HP Promo ZR2740w 27-inch LED Backlit IPS Monitor

Early Warning Deliverable

From Section 7.1, the following example of a pushed metric deliverable to a targeted audience is also an example of linked data. The reader could click on the headline contained in the Global Information Snapshot for the security analyst abstract or opinion as well as go directly to the news source for further details.

GLOBAL INFORMATION SNAPSHOT Tuesday, October 5, 2004		
Africa		
South Africa		
Terrorism	The government feared al-Queda operatives may be hiding out in Muslim theological schools, known as Darul Ulooms.	Cape Argus
Asia Pacific		
Asia Pacific		
Crime	Heavily armed pirates attacked two tugboats, which operate out of Singapore in the Malacca Strait last week, boarding the vessels with guns firing. The pirates took documents and valuables and kidnapped some of the crew.	Straits Times
Australia		
Social	Thousands of demonstrators marched in cities across Australia in protest at the country's Unrest role in Iraq, less than a week before a general election. The future of about 850 Australian troops in the Gulf became an important issue in the campaign.	BBC
India		
Political	Authorities in Delhi asked the US to withdraw sanctions against two Indian scientists whom Washington said sold nuclear technology to Iran. Indian foreign ministry spokesman, Navtej Sarna, said the scientists, C Surender and YSR Prasad, made no such sale or transfer.	BBC

Indonesia		
Disease	Tests confirmed the entire stock of 350 chickens at a farm in Grobogan died of the H5N1 virus. This was the first time Indonesia reported bird flu infections in poultry since the disease re-emerged in Southeast Asia in 07/2004.	International SOS
Political	Outgoing President Megawati Sukarnoputri tearfully conceded defeat on 10/05/2005 in last month's elections, clearing the way for the winner to begin forming a new government.	Associated Press
Japan		
Political	Japan needs a more flexible defense policy to allow the country to better tackle new security threats including terrorist attacks, but it should not change its ban on the possession of nuclear arms, a government panel said on 10/04/2004.	Reuters
Malaysia		
Terrorism	The Home Ministry revoked the permanent resident status of 16 suspected Jemaah Islamiah members.	Straits Times
Pakistan		
Terrorism	Troops were deployed to put down a riot in the Pakistani city of Sialkot, which broke out after an attack on a mosque which killed at least 30 people.	BBC
South Korea		
Home-land Security	Police sought to set up booths inside the Customs, Immigration and Quarantine (CIQ) area of Incheon International Airport to enhance readiness for the possible entry of suspected terrorists.	Korea Times

Military	The United States agreed to delay withdrawing its troops from South Korea until 2008 following concerns by Seoul officials, a report said on 10/04/2004.	Agence France Presse
Social Unrest	About 100,000 South Koreans staged an anti-communist rally on 10/04/2004, burning North Korean flags to press their calls for the downfall of the Pyongyang government and an end of its suspected nuclear weapons programs.	Reuters
Taiwan		
Disease	The red fire ant, which can inflict a painful sting that causes blisters, and in rare cases prove fatal, infested the Taiwanese capital Taipei. Experts warned it could take up to three years to eradicate the pest.	BBC
Thailand		
Disease	Thailand earmarked more than USD140 million to eradicate avian flu and overhaul small poultry farms, which play a key role in the spread of the deadly disease.	Straits Times
Disease	Thailand said on 10/04/2004 its declaration that a dog caught the deadly bird flu was an error probably caused by a mislabeled sample.	Reuters
Political	Prime Minister Thaksin Shinawatra planned to set up a new security command to coordinate government efforts to curb violence in southern Thailand.	International SOS

Europe		
Italy		
Disease	Doctors ruled out SARS in the death of an Italian singer last week after she returned to Rome from China, where she had worked for six months.	Agence France Presse
Social Unrest	It appeared that a strike by container-transport operators in Italy that began on 09/27/2004 would continue through the first week of 10/2004. The truckers belonged to five transport organizations, and they were protesting an 8% fuel tariff increase.	FedEx
Norway		
Home-land Security	The Police Security Service and the Armed Forces responded on 09/02/2004 to the new Security threat scenario by heightening security at Norwegian train stations, embassies, and bases abroad.	Oslo Aften-posten
Russia		
Home-land Security	Airports imposed new security measures, where travelers were required to remove their shoes and coats during security checks.	Associated Press
Spain		
Home-land Security	Spain vowed to crush the Basque separatist group ETA after the arrest of an alleged leader in raids by police in France. Spanish Interior Minister Jose Antonio Alonso called the arrest of Mikel Albizu "an extremely hard blow to the terrorist gang."	BBC

Middle East		
Iran		
Political	Iranian Vice-President and outspoken reformist, Mohammad Ali Abtahi, resigned from the Islamic Republic's increasingly isolated government. President Mohammad Khatami would have to approve the resignation of Abtahi, one of eight vice presidents.	Agence France Presse
Iraq		
Advisory	Indonesia on 10/05/2004 welcomed the release of two of its nationals who were held hostage in Iraq, and reiterated earlier warnings for all its citizens to immediately leave the war-torn country.	Associated Press
North America		
Canada		
Home-land Security	Reducing traffic bottlenecks at busy border points without sacrificing efforts to screen out terrorists will be a prime focus when US Homeland Security Director Tom Ridge visits Ottawa, Ontario next week.	Toronto Star
Social Unrest	Stelco Inc., Canada's second-largest steelmaker, said the union representing workers at its Lake Erie facility issued a notice of a potential strike within 90 days.	Bloomberg
United States		
Disaster	Mount St. Helens released more steam on 10/04/2004 following several days of tremors and low-level earthquakes that raised fears that the mountain might blow at any moment.	Associated Press

Military	US Defense Secretary Donald Rumsfeld cast doubt on whether there was ever a relationship between Saddam Hussein and al Qaeda.	Associated Press
Terrorism	US authorities brought charges on 10/04/2004 against Saajid Badat, a British citizen, who they contend conspired with admitted al-Queda member, Richard Reid, to use shoe bombs to blow up planes in midair.	Associated Press
South America		
Argentina		
Social Unrest	On 10/04/2004 at 1100 local time, members of the APEL picketing group marched through the center of the capital city of Buenos Aires in protest of their wages.	Air Security International
Ecuador		
Social Unrest	On 10/04/2004, beginning at 0700 local time, hospitals and health clinics nationwide halted all services, except emergency services, as part of a strike called by the health workers union.	Air Security International
South America		
Border	Continuing media coverage of suspected international terrorist links in the so-called tri-border area between Argentina, Brazil, and Paraguay continued to fuel speculation of terrorist activity in the area, particularly in Ciudad del Este.	Control Risks Group

Venezuela		
Military	Venezuela was looking to buy arms to strengthen its military capability, and Russian MiG-29 fighters were among the options being evaluated, a senior officer said on 10/04/2004.	Reuters
Political	The United States said on 10/04/2004 it will seek better ties with oil-rich Venezuela in the clearest sign since President Hugo Chavez won a recall referendum in 08/2004 that Washington was looking for reconciliation with the firebrand populist.	Reuters

JMP PRO Connections: The Transversality of the Capability Maturity Model

In this appendix we will visit the following points:

1. The Tangential concept versus the Transversal Maturity Model mode
2. Business Case Outline to map transversal concepts to JMP
3. From univariate process control to multivariate with something in between
4. Process screening, the bridge between univariate and multivariate monitoring
5. Transversal maturity space in relation to JMP PRO features

Changing the abstraction or perception of the maturity model is important for making the "CONNECTIONS" with JMP PRO. As the data and semantic competency of your organization that uses information matures, we intend to show that the levels illustrated in Figures 1.1 and 1.2 as three-dimensional cubes are more than just tangential to each other as illustrated in Figure G.1.

G.1 TANGENTIAL CONCEPT

The methodology described by the Capability Maturity Model as accomplished step by step through the levels is a set of reference points on the way to achieving best practices within the enterprise. The technical personnel, statisticians, and business consumers of the key performance indicators work toward a mature competency. They will gain expertise with the JMP software as interactive users and as persons that write script to repeat analysis on new data or for automating analytical outputs. When people become subject matter

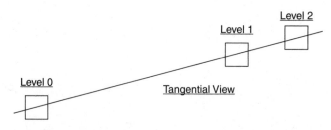

Figure G.1 Tangential View

experts in regard to both their data and the features available in JMP PRO, they will discover the hidden subtle illuminations not often written about in books or blogs; however, when the bright idea dawns on one it will seem obvious. This Appendix will communicate a golden example, saving time and effort by utilizing new features available in JMP. One can think about cube transition in the form as being transversal.

G.2 TRANSVERSAL CONCEPT

Once again, we rely on the language of mathematics to conceptualize basic facts about the various levels of maturity. The levels and their various parts are not tangential, meaning information that is merely touching or slightly connected. Their domain space edges do not simply touch each other as an organization matures from Level 0 to Level 1 through Level 3. Consequently, once the maturity takes place, the area defined by the level's intersect may have a differential topology as visualized in Figure G.2 and thus the word *transversality* best exemplifies this notion. Very much the opposite of *tangency* even though as suggested to gain maturity in our capability, we become

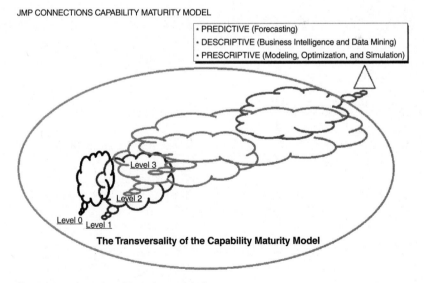

JMP CONNECTIONS CAPABILITY MATURITY MODEL

• PREDICTIVE (Forecasting)
• DESCRIPTIVE (Business Intelligence and Data Mining)
• PRESCRIPTIVE (Modeling, Optimization, and Simulation)

Level 3

Level 2

Level 0 Level 1

The Transversality of the Capability Maturity Model

Figure G.2 Transversal Maturity Model View

programmed as though it is a step-by-step process, and of course in many ways it is to fully realize the domain space. Once fully immersed in deployed capabilities reaching, for example, a Level 2 maturity, one can understand the relations and dependencies between their respective developed spaces. The overlay or intersect concept changes thinking and is what allows the organization to leverage their data assets.

If one agrees with the notion these spaces can intersect, the problem then becomes how knowing this information can be applied by JMP in certain statistics scenarios.

In a generic overview of maturity, data aggregation was an important first step along with perhaps cleaning or preparing the data sets for use in JMP. As the key performance indicators are refined and, where possible, generate analysis on-demand or via automated scripting, it brings the organization to an even higher level of maturity in a more or less bootstrap means of achievement. One common scenario familiar to everyone is process control in many differing enterprises. The cookie factory was an example where statistical process control plays an important role in manufacturing processes. One can easily relate to making cookies in one's own kitchen, small scale following a well-known recipe. If the cookies do not turn out according to the recipe, it is relatively simple to figure out where you went wrong. Now if you want to make five million cookies on an annual basis, the enterprise probably cannot afford to make mistakes on a commercial scale. So, statistical process control in the factory is crucial. As businesses change, so must the evolution of their maturity described in the following scenario.

G.3   UNIVARIATE TO MULTIVARIATE PROCESS CONTROL

Fortunately, the cookie factory has reached a maturity level to where they are getting data sets for critical control parameters as well as noncritical operating parameters and everyone is happy. They have graphs, control charts, and overlays for 300 parameters almost on a real-time basis for some subprocesses. Since businesses are always dynamic, the cookie factory takes a license from a well-known pastry chef to manufacture a new cookie. The process to make the cookie is very complex. New equipment is required; training personnel and a quality metric must be met. Licensing requires assurances to the chef for his reputation in terms of the quality of the final product since the chef's name name is on the cookie box. While the factory maturity level can handle the new product, they estimate the number of statistical process control parameters will increase by 150 for a total of 450 data points to be monitored for each batch.

All of a sudden no one is happy! Production is complaining there are too many charts to review. The process monitoring team is concerned about setting limits on parameters without the historical data to evaluate what the criteria for limits should be. And, management is concerned that cycle times or production schedules will be interrupted if there is a serious parameter that went out of specification requiring a root cause investigation.

What is an organization to do? The organization can retrospectively reference their capability maturity model. A cross functional group of people would be discussing the current state or status of capability among production subject matter experts, statisticians, process monitoring analysts, and business managers. Given the facts and their current state of maturity realization, the statistical process monitoring is totally univariate presently for the cookie factory. It is suggested that in order to get to the next level of capability in support of a new cookie manufacturing process, the company needs to start using multivariate statistical process control and monitoring. Given the maturity of their data sets, the multivariate is a viable solution.

Thus, one can see where the various defined maturity spaces intersect such that without the differential topology of transversality across the maturity levels, JMP multivariate might not be a consideration. Because of the relationships between maturity level accomplishments, we have the following opportunities:

1. Data aggregation and virtualization exists for prepared data sets at early stages of maturity.
2. JMP scripts written to automatically process hundreds of parameters.
3. Well-understood univariate level of monitoring current processes.

4. Potential savings in a reduction in number of univariate charts by maturing to multivariate controls.

5. Visualize how multiple parameters can impact each other.

In other words, identify principal factors or components that have the correlation between the variable's values and the best predictions that can be computed linearly from the predictive variables.

G.4 JMP PROCESS SCREENING

There is an initial increased cost associated with moving up the curve in the Figure 1.3 reference model. While one can assume the data is available, typically an investment is required to develop the data models for each of the processes where multivariate monitoring is required. Additional work includes validating the model and making sure it is updated if at any point in time the process changes. For some businesses, this might be a question of affordability preventing them from taking this next step. The same roadblock may apply later on if and when a company gets to the point of utilizing JMP predictive analytic features.

The good news is that JMP has a feature that would support the transversality notion in our reference model. Here is the bright idea that can save time and money in the meantime while rolling out an advanced cookie manufacturing process. The JMP PRO "Process Screening" feature in the Analyze Screening enables process monitoring by loading variable parameters across your entire process and immediately gives the viewer a *stability ratio*, a reference that tells you in a glance how things are performing within a process. The stability ratio for a parameter is to 1, the more stability that aspect of the process imparts to the viewer. Process Screening requires no initial investment. This single feature in JMP facilitates discovery on several levels. First, it is possible to deemphasize or reduce the number of univariate charts by looking at the historical data on a parameter whereby screening shows it to be very stable over time. Second, rather than loading in 450 parameters into Process Screening, subsets are chosen leading to those parameters that might be important for use in a multivariate data model. Dimensionality reduction is the process of reducing the number of random variables under consideration for obtaining a set of principal variables. Usually our variables are not so much random as they are chosen for what is considered important for monitoring a process. Process Screening in effect, one may unconsciously be doing reduction, yet in reality by taking data subsets we are dividing data into feature selections on the process and feature extraction. If multivariate analysis is pursued through data reduction, a set of parameters for building a model can be well on its way.

The Process Screening feature has many of the other JMP tools quickly available such as graphs, control charts, and shift detection. Digging even deeper, Process Capability is also built in with histograms, goal plots, capability box plots, and capability index plots.

In terms of savings, a single person can review the current status of an ongoing manufacturing process to identify any problem areas and reach out to the appropriate process monitoring experts for help on a just-in-time basis with the result of reducing FTEs. As an intermediate step between univariate process monitoring and the desire to do multivariate, working with the Process Screening might forgo multivariate all together or it could allow getting to a multivariate process monitoring state at a lesser up-front investment expenditure.

As data sets become mature, more refined, understood, and available to wider groups of people in the enterprise, the more the data sets are utilized. Often, utility stand-alone–type scripts are written and naturally proliferate because the burden of data set preparation has been removed from the end user of the data. While user engagement is a good indicator of successful maturity model implementations, even these types of activities may need to be reviewed and managed from time to time. A good example of these activities might be a handful of computed parameters derived from the existing data. If it is possible to alleviate a data entry person from having to do the calculation on a parameter and let the computer return a result, the quality of the data has improved simply by eliminating a potential mistake in calculation or a data entry error (i.e., human error).

Just like weather conditions constantly change, so do the maturity space dynamics and the data quality, and as a result getting that data into the Process Screening gives a refreshed picture of what is going on within the process of making cookies. One can determine if there is a trend, whether there is a problem in the downstream or upstream part of the process, and quickly refine the screening by adding or removing selected parameters for analysis. If an abnormal picture emerges, the idea is to be able to detect the problem while in process for correction. As is so often the case, the data may reflect a change in the process whether intentional or not. For example, the process monitoring team might decide to make a minor adjustment in the process such as the timing of adding an ingredient, an adjusted amount, and the rate added of said amount over a given mix time. As soon as the data is available from a batch the next day, the Process Screening may quickly show if the change had an impact for better or worse as well as if the change had an effect on another dependent variable parameter. What the monitoring team really wants to know from screening is if the assumptions they made for making a process change validate their reasoning, calculations, or thought processes.

G.5 TRANSVERSAL MATURITY SPACE IN RELATION TO JMP PRO FEATURES

As a process monitoring team becomes more fluent with Process Screening given this is part of the JMP Predictive and Specialized Modeling, it allows one to bring together a picture of the stability ratio and the process capability, or Ppk, in what is known as the Process Performance Graph. Thus, taken from the JMP literature and documentation (https://www.jmp.com/support/help/13/Process_Screening.shtml), a typical graphic is shown in Figure G.3.

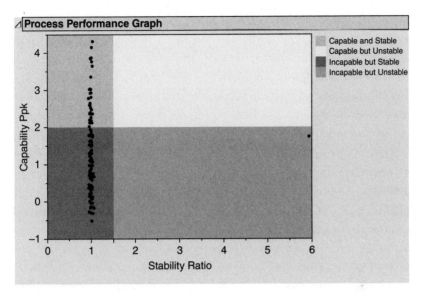

Figure G.3 Office Temperature Study

While this graph's data depicts the well-known office temperature study at JMP offices, what is important is the four quadrants. A stability ratio that exceeds 1.5 indicates that the process is unstable. A Ppk that is smaller than 2.0 indicates that the process is not capable.

The Process Screening waypoint can help clarify what subprocess components are good candidates for multivariate statistical process control where perhaps only two or three models need to be developed for critical steps such as batch enzyme, yeast, or fermentation reactor tank processes. Eliminating the guesswork and estimating the cost of creating those models makes it more palatable for management and once again escalates the capability maturity for operations and the business intelligence overall.

The Capability Maturity Reference chart in Figure 1.3 is a steep curve to climb both visually and semantically speaking in terms of actually achieving an apex of predictive, descriptive, and prescriptive analytical results. If anything can be said about the path along the way, the transversality of an organization's maturity space in correlation with

JMP PRO features shows that not only is the process under control, it also enables CPI (continuous process improvement) and continuous process verification (CPV). CPV is the collection and analysis of end-to-end production components and processes data to ensure product outputs are within predetermined quality limits, an important factor to prove compliance is maintained within the scope of the license agreement with the chef's recipe. The ongoing Process Screening aids in explaining trends and excursions from alarmed parameters with limits, and if nothing else forces an investigation to understand and bring a process back under control.

G.6 SUMMARY

In summation, a maturation toward making better mental connections with data through JMP PRO is the basis on which good business decisions are made. In efforts to arrive at and achieve each plateau of competency, a stepwise refinement process works with the goal and desire of implementation. At some point as data sets mature, as JMP scripting codifies our knowledge and the knowledge assets grow, the idea of transversality leads to efficiency in human intellectual work product. This Appendix highlights discovery possibilities awaiting a business competency center team.

References

[1] Blender. http://www.blender.org/.

[2] Gimp. http://www.gimp.org/.

[3] Git. http://git-scm.com/.

[4] Inkscape. http://www.inkscape.org/.

[5] Process Safety Management of Highly Hazardous Chemicals (CFR 1926 .64). https://www.osha.gov/doc/outreachtraining/htmlfiles/psm.html, 1996. Occupational Health & Safety Administration.

[6] Mitre Systems Engineering (SE) Competency Model, version 1. The MITRE Institute. https://www.mitre.org/sites/default/files/publications/10_0678_presentation.pdf, September 2007, pp. 47–48.

[7] Data Historians for Incident and Deviation Management. http://literature .rockwellautomation.com/idc/groups/literature/documents/wp/ftalk -wp010_-en-e.pdf, 2010. Rockwell International, Inc.

[8] Lisa Arthur. What Is Big Data? *Forbes*, 2013. http://www.forbes.com/sites/lisaarthur/2013/08/15/what-is-big-data.

[9] Salvatore Aurigemma and Raymond R. Panko. *Taxonomy of Spreadsheet Errors. Decision Support Systems*, 2010.

[10] Mike Bergman. Peg Goes Live with Broad Slate of Community Well-being Indicators. AI3, 2013. http://www.mkbergman.com/1697/peg -goes-live-with-broad-slate-of-community-well-being-indicators/.

[11] Jochen Rode, Bernhard Wolf, and Gerald Mofor. Use Cases and Concepts for 3D Visualisation in Manufacturing. http://subs.emis.de/LNI/Proceed -ings/Proceedings110/gi-proc-110-060.pdf, 2013. European Mathematical Information Service, http://www.emis.de/.

[12] Halliburton Corporation. Health, Safety and Environment (HSE) & Service Quality (SQ). Halliburton, 2013. http://www.halliburton.com/en-US /about-us/hse-sq.page?node-id=hgeyxt64.

[13] Microsoft Corporation. Compliance Features in the 2007 Microsoft Office System. Regulatory and compliance whitepapers, 2006. http://office .microsoft.com/en-us/excel-help/redir/XT010224751.aspx?CTT=5& origin=HA010224413.

[14] Microsoft Corporation. Spreadsheet Compliance in the 2007 Microsoft Office System. Regulatory and compliance white papers, 2006. http:// office.microsoft.com/en-us/excel-help/redir/AM010225682.aspx? CTT=5&origin=HA010224413.

[15] Oracle Corporation. Federated Storage Engine Overview. MySQL 5.5 Reference Manual, 2013. http://dev.mysql.com/doc/refman/5.5/en/federated-description.html.

[16] Leo J. Daconta, Michael C. Obrst, and Kevin T. Smith. *The Semantic Web—A Guide to the Future of XML, Web Services, and Knowledge Management*. Wiley Publishing Inc., Indianapolis, Indiana, 2003.

[17] Judith R. Davis and Robert Eve. *Encyclopaedia of Occupational Health and Safety*, volume II. International Labour Office, Geneva, 1998.

[18] Dr. Doug Engelbart. Doug Engelbart Institute. http://www.dougengelbart.org/about/collective-iq.html.

[19] Wayne W. Eckerson. How to Create and Deploy Effective Metrics. http://tdwi.org/research/2009/01/bpr-1q-performance-management-strategies.aspx, 2009. The DataWarehouse Institute.

[20] John F. Raffensperger. The Art of the Spreadsheet. http://john.raffensperger.org/ArtOfTheSpreadsheet/index.html.

[21] Richard C. Linger, Harlan D. Mills, and Alan R. Hevner. *Principles of Information Systems Analysis And Design*. Academic Press, Harcourt Brace Jovanovich, New York, 1986.

[22] Priyadarshi Hem. Pits & Quarries. http://technology.infomine.com/reviews/pitsandquarries/welcome.asp?view=full.

[23] Project Management Institute. PM Body of Knowledge PMBOK Guide Books. http://www.pmi.org/PMBOK-Guide-and-Standards.aspx.

[24] Dr. David Noble and Dr. Michael Letsky. Cognitive-based Metrics to Evaluate Collaboration Effectiveness. *Office of Naval Research & Evidence Based Research, Inc.*, 2000. Air University, the Intellectual and Leadership Center of the Air Force.

[25] V. Latorre and M. Roberts. KPIs in the UK's Construction Industry: Using System Dynamics to Understand Underachievement. http://redalyc.uaemex.mx/src/inicio/ArtPdfRed.jsp?iCve=127612575007, 2009. Pontificia Universidad Católica de Chile.

[26] Natalya F. Noy and Deborah L. McGuinness. Ontology Development 101: A Guide to Creating Your First Ontology. http://protege.stanford.edu/publications/ontology_development/ontology101-noy-mcguinness.html.

[27] Raymond R. Panko. Spreadsheet Research (SSR). http://panko.shidler.hawaii.edu/ssr/.

[28] Raymond R. Panko. What We Know About Spreadsheet Errors. *Journal of End User Computing*, University of Hawaii, 1998.

[29] Doug Robinson and Jordan Hiller. JMP versus JMP Clinical for Interactive Visualization of Clinical Trials Data. SAS Institute, Cary, NC, 2013.

[30] Particle Sciences. Process Analytical Technology (PAT). Technical Brief, 2012, Volume 7, 2012. http://www.particlesciences.com/news/technical-briefs/2012/process-analytical-technology.html.

[31] Marko Paavel, Sergei Kaganski, Aleksei Snatkin, and Kristo Karjust. Selecting the Right KPIs for SMEs Production with the Support of PMS and PLM. http://www.ijsk.org/uploads/3/1/1/7/3117743/8_product_life_management.pdf, 2013. International Journal of Research in Social Sciences.

[32] Wickham Skinner. The Focus Factory. *Harvard Business Review*. http://hbr.org/1974/05/the-focused-factory/ar/1, May 1974.

[33] Jeanne Mager Stellman. *Data Virtualization*. Nine Five One Press, 2011.

[34] Willbann D. Terpening. *Statistical Analysis for Business Using JMP*. SAS Institute, Inc., Cary, North Carolina, 2011.

[35] M.J. Riley, V. Lattore, and M. Roberts. Development of a System Dynamics Framework for KPIs to Assist Project Managers' Decision-Making Processes. http://www.redalyc.org/articulo.oa?id=127619214005, 2010. Pontificia Universidad Católica de Chile.

[36] Fu-Kwun Wang. Applying a Control Chart to the Learning Curve in TPM Adoption. *Quality Technology & Quantitative Management (QTQM)*, 2(2):237–48, March 2005.

[37] W. Lee and F. K. Wang. Learning Curve Analysis in Total Productive Maintenance. *International Journal of Management Science*, pp. 491–99, June 2001.

[38] Gregory H. Watson. Cycles of Learning: Observations of Jack Welch. American Society for Quality, 2001. http://asq.org/pub/sixsigma/past/vol1_issue1/cycles.html.

[39] John J. Wubbel. Foundations in Decision Process Improvement. http://www.johnwubbel.com.

Suggested Reading

For additional business justification for building a data virtualization platform, authors Judith R. Davis and Robert Eve published a good book to reference titled *Data Virtualization: Going Beyond Traditional Data Integration to Achieve Business Agility* [17]. The book speaks to sound business reasons for considering an investment in utilizing your data. It does not get too technical with respect to how to implement their ideas.

For the serious business student of statistics, a great student guide authored by Willbann D. Terpening titled *Statistical Analysis for Business Using JMP* focuses on the software that is the central component to the virtualized platform that is JMP [34]. The book will take you beyond spreadsheet fundamentals for illustrating exactly the power available in converting mere data into actionable knowledge.

For an easy guide to OEE, Exor International ("Exor") published a white paper titled "Simple Guide To OEE" that can be downloaded at: http://www.exor-rd.com/webpage?ReadForm_wPageName=products _c=Marquees.

Index